Archives of Awakening
A Loving Invitation to Look Within

Archives of Awakening
A Loving Invitation to Look Within

By Charles Rentz

Modern Enlightenment Foundation
Publishing Division
Dayton, Ohio 45420
www.ModernEnlightenmentFoundation.org

© 2017 Charles Rentz
All rights reserved.

No part of this publication may be reproduced, distributed, or transmitted in any form or my any means, including photocopying, recording, or other electronic or mechanical methods, without the prior written permission of the publisher.

9 8 7 6 5 4 3 2 1

First Edition
Printed in the United States of America

Library of Congress Cataloging-in-Publication Data
Rentz, Charles
Archives of Awakening: A Loving Invitation to Look Within
1. Spirituality. 2. Spiritual Life. 3. New Thought. I. Title
p.cm.
2017904098

ISBN 978-0-9862276-2-2 (paperback)

Cover and interior design by Integrated Marketing Logic, Graphic Design Division.

CONTENTS

Introduction vi

The One Who Sees 2

It is Time 5

Our New Earth - A Collective Journey 7

The Choice is Always Yours 10
Mindfulness Meditation

Life - A Journey of Awakening 12

Stay the Course 15

Expect Now 16

Breaking Through - A Variety of Prose 18

Now Mantra 23

Your Story of Now 24

Life is a Choice 32

Presence Meditation 34

Your Boundless Nature 36

Quotes I 41

Collective Reality - A New Year's Awareness 45

You are Already That Which You Are Seeking 49

A Glimpse of Passion 51

We Are All Here 54

Accepting Reality 55

If it's not Joy - It's not Me. 57

Embodiment of Grace 63

Conditioned or Conscious Courage 64

My Human Friends 66

No Reason 69

Open Your Eyes Now 70

Shedding Layers of Delusion 72

Look Inward 75

My Ego, My Friend, Good Bye 76

The Gift of Life - Rejoice NOW!!! 79

The Changeless - Meditative Self Inquiry 80

Your Answers are Within 89
Contemplation Meditation

Beyond the Veil of Vanity 99

You Are Wherever You Go 101

Honoring Earth - The Bearer of Truth 102

You Are the Difference 106

Acceptance and Egoic Games...............................107

Truth - Knowing the Unknown.............................112

The Power of Belief...114

Watch the Thinker...122

Random Prose 129

Sadness, My Teacher, Thank You 132

Our Collective Human Family..............................133
One Earth - One Community

Misunderstanding Presence 139

Quotes II..141

Realizing Untruth..144

Parents - Forgive Yourselves.................................146
You are bearing the same wounds as
your children

The Myth of Self and Suffering 154

A Guru's Parable...159

Uncertainty..161

Letting Go of the Story of We...............................162

About the Author...175

Introduction

Archives of Awakening is a collection of literature written in various forms by Charles Rentz amidst his distance-less journey of awakening, as clarity of consciousness was revealed. With the exception of the first few pieces of this book, the literature is arranged quite randomly, and does not reflect a timeline or reading strategy. Spiritual awakening appears to be quite beautifully random which means: not every piece will resonate with one's inner being at a particular time in their life. Yet, many may discover that something you read today, which may not offer an 'a-ha' moment, when reread two years later, has great resonance with your being.

Charles states, "There is no story here; no drama, no fantastical accounts, no philosophy, and nothing to believe in. Only words arranged in various structures filtered through my humanness, as dictated by the seed of consciousness within my being, as my being, through by being. This book is not a piece of entertainment, not an event, but a tool or pointer to find your answers from within. Please see: You are the answer. In fact, no reading is necessary to realize your true nature."

Once words find their way to paper or screen in the

INTRODUCTION

form of sentences, something amazing happens. A profound clarity begins to immerge. Charles shares, "Many times, when I went back and reread what was written, it was as if I was reading it for the first time. It was consciousness doing the writing from within, sending a message to focus upon."

Virtually all human beings, at some time or another, become aware of something greater within, often in the form of profound internal verbal messages. However, if the message is not captured on paper, screen, or recording, due to our inability to hold our attention in one place (for very long), the inner note of wisdom immediately gets lost among other countless mind streams, negative self talk, and unconscious voices. Those profound messages, when they arise, are pointers to truth radiating from within and directing us inwards – to the very essence of which we are seeking; yet, remarkably so, we rarely have the awareness, attention span, self honesty, and consistent environment to notice; and, if we do not utilize our capabilities to notice our inner wisdom, then we certainly will not be able to use that guidance to awaken.

Whether or not one is consciously aware, deep within every being is yearning to be free of suffering – a natural desire to liberate one's self – to find your true nature – peaceful stillness, as grace.

Who doesn't want to be happy? Yet, when we look out into the world, or more importantly, within, fear seems to be growing. What could possibly be the problem? Is the happiness we are seeking non existent? Or, is it possible that we have forgotten, and have never known the truth of happiness, because we have been deeply conditioned to rely only on the mind-made conditionality of emotions, for temporary moments of fleeting glee; meaning: we are stuck in a cycle of happy times followed by bad times and vice versus. It appears we are identified so deeply with mind that we think happiness can only be experienced through the realm of thoughts, feelings, sensations, memories, and emotions; and, believe that that is the only way to exist in human form.

Is it possible, we have never directed and focused our attention deeply enough, inward, towards the essence of our truest nature – an unconditional existence as pure presence, pure awareness, our core being, which watches the play of life beyond judgment, accusations, criticism, and blame…beyond the physical dimension of existence? Underneath mind?

Is it possible we are, in fact, asleep, in a trance, unconscious to our very nature – blind to stillness lying dormant underneath many veils of conditioning…until, one honestly and consciously chooses to awaken? Are you already that which you are seeking? Are you already that which you are seeking from…but simply are not aware? Are you open to this possibility? Are you open to the possibility there is another way to exist beyond suffering, beyond identity – beyond all ego constructs – even beyond your spiritual ego?

INTRODUCTION

Have we been so intensely conditioned that we are lost in compulsive thinking; lost in illusory layers of content, concepts, ideas, intellect, and belief systems...all of which are manufactured by mind? Is the answer we are seeking deeply muddled in always trying to figure things out...stuck in analysis paralysis? Is it possible we are unconsciously lost in 'wanting' more content, data, and information, which continually piles on top of our obsession for more knowledge? While seeking to find that place of consistent peace along our spiritual journey, in pursuit of ending suffering, could all of the pining for more information, more knowledge, more ideas, and content, actually be distracting us from the simple answer – masking what is right here now? What if there are no answers that can be learned, figured out, or imagined? What if the answers we are seeking must be experienced, within, without mind-made understanding? Would you be willing to look? Are you open to the possibility that what you are seeking, truth, exists without mind?

Are you ready to begin or continue listening with your heart? To experience your answers from within – underneath words – underneath mind – underneath imagination – underneath concepts and intellect?

Within this book, there is a single page which contains the most profound truth that any being could possibly convey with paper. Most everyone on earth longs for understanding truth of existence, and many seek out an enlightened spiritual master to ask, "Who am I?" In one version or another, all truly enlightened gurus share the essence of the following answer: "You are stillness. You are emptiness."

You see, with regards to true spiritual awakening, the answers we are seeking ultimately do not arrive from thinking but from observing. Neither, do our answers come in the form of words, speech, sentences, data, concepts, or content, yet through insight and realization. Ultimate truths do not come from any external other, master, or person. Your answers are within – you are the answer. Masters only use words, messages, and questions to help us seek inward – using meditative self inquiry – to rediscover and discover the answers which are already there – here now. The portals of spiritual understanding really begin opening when one is able to discern the difference between 'Listening with your heart.' versus 'Listening with your mind.' Mind will only get one so far, but then mind made answers must be dropped.

The aforementioned page I am going to momentarily guide you towards, demonstrates the essence of truth when masters indicate that your deepest essence, (you), is emptiness, stillness, nothingness, presence, and that silence is your true nature. In my opinion, there is more truth on this single page I will direct you towards then all of the words written in this entire book. In a way, this page assists one with listening with heart – listening with deep inner being.

Ok…ask yourself this question, "What is my true nature?" then please go to the page BETWEEN 88 and 89 to

INTRODUCTION

discover your answer. (This page has no page number); there you will find a page like no other in this book. Ponder the question as you examine this page, and watch your mind. (GO there NOW then come back in a few minutes.)

Please, don't just think this empty page is a joke then immediately come back to this introduction. Honestly, allow yourself to honor and experience the essence of the invitation. Please go there again, if need be, and listen deeply…listen deeply with your heart. Of course, your mind may readily present itself in the form of a variety of tactics to block your self inquiry; for instance: negative self talk, unpleasant bodily sensations, and internal voices of resistance. Those voices, sensations, and resistance are examples of what is NOT you…simply observe them, and watch them come and go.

As you continue reading this book, I would suggest keeping this (empty page experience) with you in the forefront of your consciousness – in your heart. All the words in this book, in truth, point to that page – the page which acts as a mirror for you – to see your true essence – here now – to recognize your own answers within – beyond words, imagination, concepts, memory, intellect, and images.

You are stillness and grace manifested in human form. You are already that which you are seeking. You are already that which you are seeking from.

Listen with your heart.

*Turn inward, as witness to unspeakable
and unthinkable answers; for seeking truth
in external content, yeilds only more questions.
You are already that, which you are seeking.
You are already that, which you are seeking from.*

Archives of Awakening
A Loving Invitation to Look Within

*Be now; as you are; as timeless presence;
as grace; is the miracle that everyone must see.*

The One Who Sees

Long Version:

It is always now. There is never a time when it is not now. You ask, "What is this 'it' you are referring to?" One answers with silence. Then you ask again, "Please, what is this 'it' I sense?" One answers with stillness. Persistently, a third question beckons, "Please, tell me, what is this 'it' you are making reference to?" No one answers.

As the questioner examines the physical environment to see the one, there is no one there. The questioner raises both arms reaching to the skies - towards infinite outer space above - gasping for breath - to find words that unknowingly muddle inevitable truth - losing the very essence of what the questioner is seeking. Thus, egoic questions of who, what, when, where, why, and how of 'it,' and the 'one' ensue.

As truth begins to emerge, the questioner drops to the ground in despair...sobbing - clawing at the earth. Then, beating the physical ingredients of life with fists of despair, more awakening presents something deep within -

yearning for freedom. A sense of hysterical joy mingled with ironic horror unveils reality - for an instant. A primal scream arises from depths of interdependence of this 'one' which is not separate from ever present eternal nothingness and fullness of 'it' - "WHY!!!!"

Frantically shaking, the cloak of body begins to weaken and fall away. Tears of fear turn to joyous droplets of rain - dissolving back into 'what is' - from whence they came. The "Who am I?" passes through consciousness from unconsciousness where this question has been living...then the question is gone.

The answer seemed to be there, but the nouns and verbs are not. The reason seemed to be there, but the adjectives and adverbs are not. An indescribable knowing is sensed, but the words to share it with others, do not exist, never have, and never will.

Truth awakens further from within and profound essence of nothingness points inward to inconceivable truth - that no person could ever understand through intellect, thought, memory, or emotion. A realization, "There is no answer." But, 'it' is there - beyond belief - beyond conceptualization - beyond verbalization; 'it' is not an idea; 'it' is truth. "YES!!!!

This one here has seen it! This one here IS IT!!! This one here is - as is all - as is it - as it is...now" "I am...I AM!... I AM!!!!!"

Then..........stillness............then......nothing.......... then deeper realization.........."There is no then." A deep unshakeable peace and calm arises as truth is fully revealed. This one here sees without eyes, that it is always now - that now is it - and it is one. This one here has awakened. This one here is no longer blind. This one here no longer resists. This one here has let go - surrendered ego - given up the fight – seen itself. This one here is incapable of suffering in any form, for the one is formless. As present as the instant when innocent joy, compassion, and unconditional love breached the womb, as pure grace, yet with vast experience of unknowing, this one here sees….again. I AM all that is - I am life...I am…I… .

Short Version:

I am like a leaf in the wind...a crashing wave upon the shore...a grain of sand amidst the desert. I am nothing. I am no one. I am. I. .

It is Time

Look around on the outside with honesty and keen awareness, and you will probably see a lot of what you do NOT need. Take a look on the inside, with sincerity, compassion, and an open heart and mind, and you will discover everything you DO need – stillness, inner peace, consciousness. You will find that everything you have been searching for, out there, in the materialistic world, to end your suffering, is already here – within you. Your answers have no physical form, no tangible manifestation, no definitions, and no meaning. Your solutions come in the essence of experience – the experience of surrender – of letting go – pure grace.

To this, there is no beginning, no end, only now. You reveal the only one unchangeable truth – your authentic, unencumbered, genuine being – whom you were born as – your innocent, worthy, and deserving presence…not the child within, not the many false selves vying for dominion, not convoluted identities masked in fear, and NOT multiple layers of guilt and shame casting an illusory shadow of protection using your feelings and emotions…yet deeper seeing unveils truth – the revelation of YOU – as life…stillness.

Your suffering is within – it is yours. And it is up to you, to find it, allow it, love it, cherish it, then – put it down; perhaps grieve its loss, drop it, and walk away. Your suffering is like an old toxic friend pulling you into the abysmal chaos of despair, whom you must depart from. Your friend serves you no more.

It is time to let your companion, suffering, go. Have strength to disappoint your suffering. Allow humble truth of absolute vulnerability be seen, so truth of invulnerability can be humbly experienced - dispelling delusion. Have wisdom to see that all suffering is an illusion. Have courage to abandon your shame. Have compassion as your 'self' to be as you are. There is no dishonor in letting go what you no longer need. Be, as you are, to see that all suffering, is an illusion - as you watch it melt away into nothingness.

Embrace your truest nature. Embrace awareness. Embrace your being. Embrace life. It is time.

Our New Earth - A Collective Journey

As our new earth draws near an unrestless calm be still my timid heart. Deep within the darkest confines of my being I find my soul lurking; yearning to break free - to find the light.

It appears to be a lonely soul trapped by conditioned patterns of society's selfishness. Patterns enmeshed in my mind bound by a web of confusion and contradiction. Perhaps my soul is my truest being trying to reveal itself - the highest knowing lying dormant until courage and consciousness eclipse. Or, maybe my soul is simply me; the "I am"; my selfless self masked by many veils of ego.

Struggling to find the way in a world of delusion fueled by resistance to realities of evolution, my inevitable journey awaits. Attempting to find conscious solace by turning to unconscious adoptions of untruths in the supernatural, fiction, and unnecessary attachments only delay me. I seem to be unwilling to wholeheartedly yield to the infinitesimal building blocks of who we really are, and allow myself to be nurtured by the only real surrogate parents of life - the sun, and the earth.

Life. A journey unwillingly bequeathed to each and every one of us yet lived by only a few. All life born on a single plane of existence governed by the same relentless laws of nature. Each one of us on a voyage of survival pursuing physical and material fulfillment. We seem to deny the truth when consciously aware we need only each other, and when fully awaken, there is nothing to survive.

The higher path undertaken only by a few who choose consciousness. The few kindred spirits who embrace courage, compassion, and love to overcome millions of years of instincts. Instincts born from physical survival evolved into modern selfish wants and fully grown into a collective state of unconscious global immaturity. An unfortunate existence where most turn a blind eye to our home the earth, and our family the fellow life forms on our planet. A limited number of us have chosen to live by example - to lead, to show, to break collective mind patterns of society, and be the answer to peace on earth.

Am I wading in the stream of culture? Am I an unconscious statue of denial? Do I wield inner strength to see the truth?

Dare I wage the inner war against evolution? Dare I destroy ego that fights altruism? Dare I grapple and overcome my fear of change? Dare I live the change mandatory for the survival of humankind, life, and our planet? Dare I choose to become a peaceful warrior advocating truth?

Dare I "be" a pioneer for the birth of our new earth?

As I approach our new earth, my ego is peering from the shadows attempting to pull me away from the only truth there is, but with one glance into the luminous sky, radiant light disintegrates all doubt. As I draw closer to our new earth, my kindred family of "all fellow humans" offers me strength to overcome fear.

When I reach my destination and step away from my steel horse, I feel the ground of which I was born beneath my feet. When I am greeted by any sentient being of my human family, a mutual knowledge of "I am" and "We are" captivates and energizes me. Our unified connection softens my heart revealing and fortifying compassion, altruism, peace, and love to continue my individual quest, and our collective journey.

The Choice is Always Yours
Mindfulness Mediation

There is absolutely no reason to suffer, except those you have already made up, or looking to invent. Try this: say to yourself, "There is no reason to suffer." and see if you can hear the voices of resistance defending suffering.

Any voices you hear ARE NOT you. Any reasons that you THINK are good enough to suffer over ARE NOT facts or truth. By allowing mind to create reasons to suffer, that you adopt as beliefs and facts, then you are choosing your own suffering. Recognize you have a choice. The choice is always yours.

Mindfulness is a wonderful practice in order to restore seeing - that there is a choice. Sit in silence watching the breath sensation at the tip of your nose (go in and out), and when thoughts arise, notice them; then, compassionately let them pass, and gently bring your attention back to your breath sensation at the tip of your nose. Just continue to sit, watching, and observing, and letting go.

Do this for 5 minutes a day, preferably in the morning, before mind becomes fully engaged, when you are a little sleepy. Then, after a few weeks, increase your time by five mintes. Continue this until you are up to 30 mintes or 1 hour a day.

You may not notice the changes, right away, but this practice is proven to decrease anxiety and nervousness, while increasing clarity and inner peace. Try it and see. That way, you will know for yourself, within, your own experience, if it works. Often times, those around you, such as family and friends will notice a pleasant difference in you, before you do.

Of course, mind seems to have the job of maintaining suffering, which means: there is typically resistance to this practice. But, do yourself a favor and give it an honest chance. Sit and "Just do it." and when sitting watch the resistance arise, typically in the form of voices and unpleaseant sensations. Continue to watch without making the end of your session a goal.

For example, you are 3 minutes into your 5 minute session and major resistance arises. You tell yourself that you only have a few more minutes left and can stick it out. Please, watch both the voices of resistance and voices of support arise, then merely pass away.

Even if the resistance comes in the form of physical discomfort somewhere in the body, simply watch it arise; see how it is subtly changing and shifting. Then, simply go back to your breath. Chances are you will notice that the sensation goes away once you redirect your attention back to the tip of your nose.

Life - A Journey of Awakening

During the journey of awakening, pain and suffering are often misinterpreted as something other than what they truly are – fear. Fear of higher truth peeking through unconscious misperceptions telling us our current identity or identities we have been attached to will no longer provide the illusion of happiness any further. Actually, fear is just an illusion created by mind as a protection system, but for now, we may reject that premise, yet we must acknowledge truth as we ponder within.

As awakening provides clarity, we begin to notice another level of awareness presenting itself indicating our identities have been masquerading as impermanent emotional survival mechanisms. We catch a glimpse that the majority (if not all) of our decisions in life have been based upon a reactionary state jousting with our current life circumstances. New conscious knowing offers insight into core issues driving our behavior: fear, fear of feeling, fear of emotions, fear of sensations, fear of dying; also known in its compulsory form as suffering.

New insights offer information that catalyze major

change and shift the essence of our being providing deeper clarity; which in turn, allows emotional and spiritual maturity to proliferate.

During inevitable stages in our lives we have natural tendencies to resist the awakening process. We feel like we are breaking down when in fact we are breaking through. This resistance is ego-mind trying to avoid being seen, because when light of our awareness shines on it, then the illusion (mind) dissolves.

During the greatest periods of resistance, we may become aware that our current support systems, friends, family, employment, and or religious beliefs have been holding us back from true conscious awakening and joy. We are offered a choice – whether or not to make a conscious decision to allow profound change or transformation to ensue; and perhaps, let people, places, and things go – which may not resonate with awakening.

Painful resistance may misdirect many of us to seek some form of higher power, god, or get lost in religion, which diverts focus and accountability off of ourselves where true power of inner peace lives – within – in our hearts – grace.

New found awareness can be quite confusing. Of course, egoic resistance appears to fight every step of the way, which often times shows up as adversity to help from those vitally instrumental to supporting our inner well-being. In other words, we run away from truth, stay with individuals and family who identify with our suffering, and push away those who can guide us.

However, by confronting our fears, and admitting our current way of thinking and living may no longer be enhancing our wellbeing, we must lift our arms up to the vast cosmos in surrender, and open our hearts; we must surround ourselves with those individuals essential to refining our process towards liberation and consistent inner peace – along our journey of awakening – life.

(Please note that the word 'journey' is misleading, since you are already that which you are seeking, and you do not have to go anywhere to see it – just look within – here now. There is no distance or journey to yourself, only an illusion of separation. Everyone is always here now, no matter our geographical location or life circumstance.)

Stay the Course

When my current circumstances seem too great a burden to remain still, and inner turmoil feels too intolerable to bear, and I feel like running in the opposite direction, it usually means there is a major breakthrough occurring.

Most likely, this period of unrest is a profound shift in further awakening my true nature, and shedding of yet another layer of maladaptive identities or thought habits, which have been holding me back from discovering truth within.

These times are temporary and impermanent, and yet another step drawing me closer to inner peace – even though I must first walk through (what appears to be) the fire of awakening…stay the course.

Expect Now

Once one realizes that nothing, which is to say: no thing, no event, no achievement, no situation, no person, no idea, no thought, and no scenario will ever make you permanently happy, then you are underway with dissolving the craving which the illusion of future happiness promises (hope). Once the illusory mask of hope completely fades away, you will be left with nothing but the eternal present moment where life truly unfolds, and the real joy of living exists – suffering is no more…here now…beyond a hopeful future.

When you begin eliminating all clinging and open to the possibility, that in reality, now is the only moment that matters, then clarity arises, revealing this: The eternal present moment (presence) is the only space where non-fleeting happiness and inner peace permanently live. You begin to experience life in the here now and see the whole of existence for what it truly is, without labels, judgments, or expectations. You begin to experience life as you…and you as life.

An understanding as to the impermanence of all things,

and that of your changeless nature, will arise, thus gaining insight into what it means to make the outcome of everything the process and the process the outcome. Life, in truth, is a process with no beginning and no end. And, processes are continually and perpetually changing; therefore, lilfe has no finite result and no outcome, hence nothing to cling to.

Processes only yield more processes – impermanence; and resistance to processes is mind trying to pause process. Please see that what you really are is underneath process and form, a changeless knowing, a changeless stillness, a changeless nothingness, incapable of suffering. Yet, since thinking has most of us lost in the illusion of a resentful past and hopeful future, we may instill a non mind-made intention, a heartfelt intention, to help focus our attention on what truly is…here now.

For the moment: If you need to anticipate something, then anticipate now. If you need an outcome to work towards, then make the ever changing impermanent practical processes of life your outcome. If you need to crave something, then crave now. If you need to cling to something, then cling to now. If you need to expect something, then expect now.

Breaking Through
A Variety of Prose

Letting go of old identities does feel like dying since in a sense I am. My old identity(s), no matter how dysfunctional or maladaptive they may be, which ironically lent their beautiful nature to me in order to survive in the physical dimension of life, of which I have found delusional security for many years to decades, have reached their end.

The breaking through process evokes fear, anxiety, and panic, since part of 'my old self' (an illusion of self) is approaching a type of death – often referred to as 'dying to oneself.' Fight or flight instincts kick in and I become either angry or fall into a passive state – both of which are driven by egoic emotions that I must not resist. There is also an ironic sense of grief and sorrow over losing my old former maladjusted personae (a companion of suffering); and typically accompanied by an emotionally cleansing period of sobbing and keening. I must remember 'it will pass' – these perceptions of suffering are only temporary even though impermanent feelings of unrest seem eternal.

The progression towards letting go is very natural and although perceived and felt as extreme emotional pain, the process is 'what it is' and must be endured until this form of human nature runs its course. Often times, I feel as though I am breaking down, but I am (in fact), breaking through. Stay the course; have courage and allow compassion to radiate from within and transform the throes of despair.

I must also express compassion and loving kindness for all others who may be experiencing this process, especially when it appears every single one of us must endure, to some degree, an incomprehensible depth of suffering when breaking through to expose truth within – to see our very nature which has been ignorantly protecting itself with hardened walls of delusion.

α α α

I am not what happens to me. I am not what has happened to me nor am I what will happen to me. I do not exist separate from my experience although my ego tells me they are different – a duality – but I know better now. Although faint and slightly blurred, I see the space between me and experience shrinking – this is self realization – this is truth – this is when life begins and suffering ends. And…a very difficult and seemingly horrifying reality (for ego) to grasp is this: realizing truth is a choice. However, as I surrender to truth, courage will see me through. I am not the one who has experienced or will experience – I am non mind-made formless perpetual state of experiencing – that's all.

α α α

Soften your heart. Give yourself permission to feel – to love. Soften your heart. Let hardened layers of emotional defense weaken with your every breath. Allow yourself to accept all – even the stuff you feel ashamed of and guilty over – the things you would never share with even your closest friend…let these things go – they are not you and never were. You are not.

You are not what happened to you or what you have done. Let illusory layers of shame, guilt, fear and unworthiness, self loathing, hopelessness, and helplessness that harden your heart, dissolve - totally. Embrace aloneness in the here and now.

Suffering is only a delusion holding you back from revealing truth within – from embracing your primal innocence – your core being – your higher self. Empower your ultimate faculty of inner peace – self compassion; and allow grace to be revealed in every cell of your body. Give yourself compassion first – always – continually. Love yourself first – always – continually. Soften your heart. It is a choice to let go of the hardness or hold onto delusion. Let love radiate within and without. Let compassion radiate within and without.

α α α

You may hear a question emanating from somewhere within, "How can I survive without thought?" This appears to be a good question to the one asking; but if you can see that the one asking is the mind, the ego – that which is not you – then awareness of your truest nature begins to arise.

The truth is this: What you really are would never ask survival questions because these questions are rooted in fear of death, and your boundless nature fears nothing and never dies. Because the concept and thought of dying you are afraid of is a belief, not a reality of truth, but a non-reality manufactured by mind, please know you are neither the mind nor the believer. Watch the mind – watch the believer – awareness watching is you.

α α α

Although discovering who we are as a human species can be scary, it is also inevitable…it is natural. Life is a journey with no beginning and no end. And, in truth, a full life can be experienced in a blink of an eye without changing geographical location.

However, the word journey is misleading as are all words; since the term journey supposes a distance and distance supposes there is something that must be sought out – out there – found at a place that is not here – now. There actually is no journey to the here and now – for the here and now is always here and now and no distance exists between you and here now. The journey is an idea manufactured by mind. There is no where to go but be here now as your deepest essence of truth – stillness.

There is no gap, distance, or journey from the illusion you are currently living to what you are seeking...life itself... for life cannot be anywhere...LIFE IS EVERYWHERE! You ARE life! It is as if you are a drop of water in the ocean and insistent on finding the ocean. It is so obvious that you cannot see it – due to the reality that you are already that which you are seeking. Look inward with compassionate grace, not with your eyes, but through your eyes – with your heart centered nature.

α α α

Now Mantra

Repeat the following several times allowed, or in your head. And, watch how your inner landscape changes, merely, by repeating words which direct attention to our true nature. This is how we can use mind, rather than allowing mind to be in control. Keep in awareness, you are the one watching the continuous changing within, which is not the mind. Note, that you may feel resistance at first; but, repeat until those feelings break, giving way to space and peace.

Now. Presence, Joy-ness, Humility-ness,
Grateful-ness, Gratitude-ness. Love. Grace.

Your Story of Now

If you are identified as the physical human form, like the rest of us, you may have found yourself suffering a great deal in life, at least once. In other words, most of us have experienced an episode of despair, anxiety, depression, overwhelming grief, or loathing - which seemed to offer no end; feeling debilitated and perhaps, emotionally repressed. Possibly there was a sense of regression, too. Amidst unbearable angst, you may have sensed you are not who you think you are while your mind uncontrollably tried to justify the story of how your life has unfolded. Your mind continues attempting to fix the past and predict the future, yearning to end the suffering, but to no avail.

You ask yourself: Why is my life like this? How did my life get this way? How can I fill that void? How can I position myself in the future for a better outcome? Of course, life is unpredictable, but very few of us honestly know what unpredictability means at a self realized level. There are many uncontrollable and varying reasons, unpredictable happenstances, and exclusive combinations of life circumstances, which are completely unique to each of our lives, and become our life's story - an unconscious story.

Each of our life stories comprise of many elements, most of which are a culmination of the following narratives: the story of who we are to be, the story of what happened, the story of what if, the story of supposed to be, and so on; all of which are seeking future controllable outcomes yet anchored in the past; past wounds experienced from some degree of perceived neglect, perceived abuse, perceived disappointment, and perceived resentment.

Predominantly, our current narratives are greatly rooted in the stories of those who have raised us, from the cultural patterns surrounding our upbringing, and habitual socioeconomic influences. All of these factors have ironically molded our lives unbiasedly; which is to say: The story of your life already began before you were even born; because, there were already preconceived notions of whom you were supposed to be, before you took your first breath of life. Thus...the beginning of an unconscious story and fairytale of your life ensued - conditioning you, against your own instinctual capacity for autonomy, and defying your innate gift of free thinking. In other words, you began your life not of your own accord.

The truth is: The introduction to your story of life, and first few chapters, were already written by someone else. Then, what do you do, like most of us? You proceed through life striving to finish writing the next chapter so it makes sense and validates the prior one. We continue living in relentless persistence to justify their story for us - not our own. Let us remember not to blame, however. Please be aware: Those who raised us had stories, too - that were NOT written by them. They were written by someone else, whose life story was written by someone else. Therefore, unconscious traditional stories of life persist and are handed down to the next generation.

With fictional stories of your life's beginnings housing the first idea of how your life's story is supposed to be, then no wonder you feel inauthentic, a sense of discontent, and inner conflict, most of your life; the story isn't yours, and most of us aren't even aware of this unconscious programming. This inner conflict or internal battle seems to be a struggle against great odds - trying to continue writing the story of how your life is 'supposed to be.' And, when appropriately contemplated, we see that our greatest struggles offer memories - which are gone - never to exist again - except in our own mind. And, fond memories? When we glance into reality at a highly conscious level, your memories really never turned out to be the way your life 'was supposed to be' either; but, in reality, another disappointment, to some degree. We chock them up as fleeting moments of happiness or temporary comfort, at best.

Our stories, if we choose to seek compassionately and honestly within ourselves, are developed to sustain this substructure in our psyche; i.e. the instinctual drive for survival, and the conditioned motivation to be happy. Of course, these two systems that motivate our inner world have become interwoven where we find ourselves living in a constant state of survival - trying to keep our 'story of life' from ending or dying. We will do practically anything to maintain our 'life's story' which was designed by many false identities as characters of that story.

Therefore, we end up fighting to sustain our story of life, thus sustaining our false identities, and conditioned patterns; because they have become our survival system; or, the story of who you are - the story of "who I am."

For instance, if I am not this, then who am I? In other words, if I am not fulfilling my obligations to my story of 'supposed to be' then who am I? Am I lost in the story of 'who I was' and attempting to recreate a pattern of 'who I am to become' - in the future?

Who am I without a job? Who am I without a job title? Who am I if I don't have a significant other? Who am I without a husband - without a wife? Without a sports car? Without a lot of money? Without a college education? Who am I if I do not want to conform to maladapted patterns of society? Who am I if I no longer want to live a life written by others, and now…want to write my own - live my own life? Who am I if the people closest to me don't believe in me, and trust me to write my own story of life? Do

I let those who do not support me, go? Do I try to appease those that defy my authentic story - by playing the role that family, culture, and government have bequeathed to me - thus living the life they expect - inauthentically?

Aren't their expectations exactly the story of my life, as authored by them? And, not the story of my life, authored by me. Is it not within my capacity as an autonomous human being, who never asked to be born, to write my authentic narrative of my own life, beyond obligation?

The answer is, absolutely, of course! All of us have the perceived right to live our lives the way we want; rather, the way we mistakenly choose! But first, we must recognize that we have a choice. And, this choice masks itself in an addiction of sorts - an addiction to someone else's story of how our life is supposed to be.

Moreover, on rare occasions, we find ourselves attempting to live the life we choose, but rarely recognize we are addicted to our current life - which was honestly never written by us. And, we wonder why we suffer and are dissatisfied most of the time. Certainly, most of us have fallen into a complacent state of unconsciousness, where delusional happiness takes over - leaving us living quasi inauthentic lives. For clarity, allow me to state that most of us end up discovering a level of tolerable and pseudo comfort-ability, and stay there for our entire lives, living someone else's story; which, by the way, is NOT authentic happiness, but a state of impoverished hope. Most of us 'give up' on our own story and accept the 'make the best of it' attitude. In other words, we never 'go for it' - to write our own authentic story.

Of course, with life as an impermanent process, there is more irony that follows when we examine how our lives literally unfold. We may discover, even when writing your own story, you are still writing a story of how your life is 'supposed to be,' not what your life actually is - what your life truly is - in the here now. This mild paradox leads us to another major distinction: The first one as the distinction between your life's story written by someone else versus the one authored by you; and two: your story of life as you've written it with the 'supposed to be' theme, versus your story of now - the story you live everyday that you aren't paying attention to.

When we take a deeply compassionate yet brutally honest look at the 'story of our life' written by others, and also the story that we think we are writing for ourselves, we see that most of these narratives are rooted in the 'supposed to be' mental framework; which are nothing more than illusory future projections. We become lost planning, thinking, and strategizing how to write our own life's story – so it turns out to be the way it is supposed to be - rather than simply taking our hands off the wheel and seeing what happens - because we are too afraid.

And, when our lives don't turn out to be the way they are supposed to be, (the way we have fictitiously planned), then we suffer. In addition, and typically unbeknownst to us, we are unconsciously motivated by factors from the past - how your life WAS supposed to be. THEN, we attempt to implement tactics to recreate a story to fill the void of the past. All of these past and future mental circus acts only create more suffering. Take a look at the last few paragraphs and you will notice a theme: the theme of past and future cycling over and over leading to suffering – directly because both past and future are always non existent.

Most of us fall in love with our delusional stories of past and future, not with life as it is - our story of now. Whatever happened to the story of now? Have you ever written this story? Or, even glimpsed a fleeting notion of it - at least once, in that millisecond of: pure calm, authentic peace, and surrender - that left you awestruck and in love with life, beyond all conditions. I want you to write your story of now. I want to read it. I want to hear it! Yet, most importantly, you need to write it for yourself - while simultaneously living it.. But needing is not the same as wanting. Do you even want to write your exclusive and authentic story of now?

The story of now, which all of us unconsciously experience continually everyday, is always present, without judgment, without the fictional story of 'supposed to be' attached to it. We spend our lives unconsciously creating circumstances and life situations to fulfill our expectations of how our life is supposed to be - WITHOUT ever practicing writing our story of now. What is your story of now? Are you finished writing the fictional story of your life from the past? Are you finished writing the sci-fi fictional version of your life about the future?

Are you ready, willing, and capable of writing your story of now, now? I remember a phrase, "Get busy living or get busy dying." I translate these words as follows: Are you going to write your story of now, consciously, or continue dying unconsciously?

Choose the story of now - you deserve it! As does each and every one of us. When we begin writing our own story of now, we unlock a reality that we never knew existed. We discover that there is no factual story of past or future. We begin to realize there is only one narrative which has ever existed, and ever will - your story of now.

Life is a Choice

Life is like driving down a mountain with no brakes and an unavoidable chasm of nothingness awaits you at the bottom. You cannot turn; you cannot change direction; you cannot stop. Once one accepts the reality of this analogy in absolute conscious, then one begins experiencing life beyond the fear of dying and fictional perception – clarifying the essence of true inner peace.

Our obsessions, attachments, delusions, shame, pain, suffering, and fear of death, are powerful addictions that we must release – let go. Let go of them all. Our addictions have given our lives false meaning – something to identify with, but ultimately yield more suffering; they are nothing but mental projections of future or past that do not exist in the timeless present moment of now.

We are nothing but insignificant life forms attached to a massive rock hurtling through endless space and time until we: crash into something, burn up in the sun, nature somehow ends our existence, or we destroy ourselves; these are our options – this is our inevitable future – this is reality…and this is beautiful! Accept the finality of physical form and walk through gates of reality into the realm of now where life unfolds and uncertainty dissolves.

Fear of reality, which is to say, fear experienced from not accepting the illusory fact of death, and holding onto cautious uncertainty there is something else after we perish, only blocks truth of immortality – creating more delusion; and, delusion breeds fiction – which spawns drama – and drama distracts all of us from focusing on the most important question in the universe, "Why not choose to free myself, right now, so the limited time we share together is spent relishing in loving kindness and immersed in compassion and oneness?"

Resist no more. Shed your remaining layers of denial. Let go of your fear of truth – that everything is changing – constantly – impermanent – that you wield absolutely no control. Let your highest self emanate from within and cast a light, so bright upon the earth, that everyone can experience whom you really are: pure love, pure compassion, pure being – absent of shame, guilt, blame, criticism, delusion, greed, judgment, and hatred.

When your boundless nature finally departs the paradoxical form of human life, and the body is shed back unto earth as nothing more than the mere elements which created it, let your imprint left in the hearts and minds of your fellow humans be only a message of altruistic inspiration, and loving grace, led by example.

This is a choice. Your life is a choice. Your choice.

Presence Meditation

Stay in the moment.
Everything is always alright.
It is so clear and serene here…
…just being.

Long, slow effortless breaths dissolve any unrest.

Living as timeless presence.
No anger, shame, guilt, or pain exists here…
…only peace.

*Witness the stillness between each inhalation
and exhalation.*

No comparing and no monkey mind.
Just observing - witnessing.
No concern of what others think.
Confidence in not knowing.

Listen to stillness behind all sound.

A LOVING INVITATION TO LOOK WITHIN

No judgment – only love.
No what ifs. No maybes. No should haves.
Only calm compassion and love.

Long, slow deep breaths restore life - offering peace.

No negativity. No analyzing. No impulsivity.
Every action is intentional.
No questioning why?
No questioning anything. No obsessing.

Simply watch, notice, observe inhalation and exhalation.

Peaceful simply being.
There is only one true moment, as timeless
presence, with no beginning or end.

Peaceful simply being.

Your Boundless Nature

Unto the unfathomably perfect dimension of existence, as a guest upon timeless earth, each one of us is born wielding a flawless piece of unconditional life. In truth, and bound by nothing, consciousness, as beautiful unbiased randomness mingled with perfectly balanced essence of grace, offered your being a choiceless choice. An unthinkable decision when spoken in confused physical language means something like this: We happened upon a boundful physical realm bearing indescribable capabilities beyond mind and intellect to realize truth – that we do not live life – but are life.

Momentarily tethered in physical mesh, our first inhalation becomes key witness as momentum of external conditional stimuli immediately begins masking us with unconscious protection from the abyss of infinite conscious possibilities; and what follows for an indeterminate length of time are uncertain series of breath experiences – with each breath as delicate thread gently bonding form with formlessness.

Although housing truth, infinite possibilities, however, are not available yet. How could they be? How could boundless potential arise in awareness to an innocent, worthy, and deserving infant who only seconds ago arrived in human form – as nothing more than a helpless complex of well organized soil and electrical impulses? A tiny piece of life wrapped in an interwoven bag of cells whose only option is temporary reliance on a 'conditional other' for survival.

Even now, in what we understand as adulthood, the world appears to be lost on a treadmill of illusory patterns of survival. Thought and behavioral habits bestowed upon us from the unconscious blind leading the unconscious blind. Generations of walking dead drowning in fear, guilt, and shame…addicted to innumerable belief systems of accusations, criticism, blame, and resentment. All of this craving and clinging to suffering, amounting to nothing more than mere seconds of external validation packaged in a morsel of fleeting glee – a mental chocolate when once consumed leaves only desire for more. Conveniently inconvenient outward distractions further assist the avoidance of an unspeakable truth: You are already that which you are seeking – and can only be discovered when turning inward.

What appears to be opposite of truth is resistance, a survival mechanism, although two sides of the same mysterious coin. Yet in truth, there is no coin and nothing to survive, and never was and never will be for no reason at all, but if you are seeking reason: Because there never was a 'was' and never was a 'will be.' There is only now – as presence – formless nothingness – which exists as unbiased intelligence of creation living within you – which paradoxically (or ironically speaking) does not belong to you. There is no irony or paradox in truth really, but only illusion of such, for all that is – is – beyond mind-made irony or paradox.

Truth is only paradoxical and ironical to the thinker who is trying to understand, intellectualize, and figure out with relentless compulsion to know – to be protected. But knowing is only known when mind is dropped, set aside, or simply watched; then, the possibility of unknowing is revealed. For truth, the truest essence of life is the one who watches, notices, and observes: thought, sensation, and emotion…everything within and without.

Of course, there is resistance to seeing beyond the physical. A mental dissonance opposed by beautiful ego to embrace the non physical and allow the unseen to be seen; a possibility to consciously glance into the only dimension available NOT with your eyes, but THROUGH your eyes. A dimension of truth which is always here, infinitely ubiquitous, like a droplet of rain among water surrounded by oceans who does not know it is the ocean when lingering in a cloud. In a way it has gone but never left. This is truth. This is you.

Can you hear your mind screaming in rage, or protesting with bodily quivers, or merely muttering in melancholy surrender, words carrying defensive meaning like:

"I am something! I am somebody! I do matter! I have goals! I want to be heard! I do have purpose! What is the meaning of life? Why am I here? Who am I?"

Profoundly deeper yet, can you sense a voiceless voice constantly answering from behind the brick walls you have built around your heart…with fear, guilt, and shame as mortar? Amidst the ancient ruins of wonderful feelings, beautiful sensations, and glorious emotions, as the illusory walls begin to dissolve do you sense your truest nature – your core being as grace, calmly, humbly, lovingly revealing truth, with incapable words such as these:

> Becoming something is limited – you are limitless. When you matter you bound yourself. You do not matter – you are boundless. There is nothing wrong with you and never was and never will be – no matter what you think or do or have done. There is no meaning of life but only life. You ARE life. You are here for no reason at all; for with reason follows bias as an indentured servant of suffering who births the wrath of judgment – perpetually strengthening the circle of despair.

In truth, boundless nature we call life has no reason, no bias, no judgment – only love. For life, creation, what ever you haphazardly define it cannot have a reason or nothing could exist for even a single moment. True love is unconditional, now, void of judgment – an empty space of stillness – pure silence. This is you but not as form – not as an object – yet as the subject…the embodiment of grace – the end of duality. An indescribable you which can not be understood by mind but only by itself…beyond words and action.

Can you hear THIS voice? The voiceless voice of consciousness patiently awaiting; yet, with intensity so great and powerful and full of infinite potential and joy – the possibility to experience itself – as itself. Are you willing to direct your attention inward with effortless effort capable of witnessing pure silence within – so you can sense voiceless voice of truth – as you – as your boundless nature…?

Quotes I

The moment I honestly admitted to myself how
unconscious I was – was the exact same moment
I began to awaken.

α

Being human isn't easy so let's comfort and love one another (especially children) every chance
we get – we are all here.

α

It is not that you don't know who you are. The challenge
is that you are constantly trying to be someone else.

α

Crying as a release into surrender appears to be the most
honest form of emotional cleansing and manifested expression for letting go of resistance.

α

There is no such thing as independence,
only interdependence.

α

Mind wants to guilt and shame you away from
accepting help, when the truth is: no one can live
in the physcial realm very long without it.

α

Inner peace is a choice.

α

I don't know what will happen and
neither does anyone else.

α

Pay attention to how everything is perpetually
changing, except one thing...awareness.

α

You can only learn to become; It is impossible
to learn to be. You can only try to become;
it is impossible to try and be.
Drop becoming. Drop trying. Be.

α

If it feels separate, it's not me.

α

Accepting help is as great of a gift as giving it.

α

Dropping urgency attached to everything external in your
life will reveal what is truly important within.

α

Spiritually speaking with reference to ending suffering, it
appears to be more efficient to let go of who you are not,
than spending your entire life searching and trying to figure out who you are; for no other reason than this: There
never was a mind-made self to begin with.

α

Your answers are within.

α

A LOVING INVITATION TO LOOK WITHIN

The most loving and honest form of communication is silence.

α

A great step in awakening is having the ability to know when you are thinking for yourself and when you are not. In other words, to know when you are using your mind versus when your mind is using you.

α

A wonderful discernment is to realize: whatever you do or have done is NOT who you are.

α

The human mind body complex is a powerful machine whose sole biological purpose is to survive and whose primary psychological purpose is to label and attach meaning to everything. You are not your body, not your mind, not your emotions, not your memories, not your sensations, not your feelings…you just are.

α

I am not the body, not the mind, not the emotions, not the memories, not the sensations, not the feelings…I am not.

α

Your conscious existence always begins here now – for existence is already here and your conscious life is already now – you are consciousness.

α

There is no excitement, urgency, or expectation, (in spiritual truth so to speak), yet only peace – a deep sense of grace – an unshakable calm. And, that's how you know (through direct experience) you are on the path that has no right or wrong – the distanceless path of here-now – guiding effortlessly beyond pace, direction, and illusion of time.

α

Here is incapable of being a geographical location. Now is incapable of being a moment in time.

α

Englightenment is not a destination.

α

If you find yourself rushing to meditation or yoga, then you are missing the point. If you find yourself rushing anywhere, then you are, most likely, missing your life.

α

Ask yourself, "What am I willing to let go of for inner peace?"

α

If I think someone or something external is causing my suffering, then I may need to let go of accusations, criticisim and blame, and review my of projections arising from self judgment.

α

'Divine will' is the absence of 'personal will' - to be here now - as you are - void of the illusion of control.

Collective Reality
A New Year's Awareness

Yet once again, in our patterns of existence and human communication, the pages of time have turned that many of us label, 'A New Year.'

"Happy New Year!" resonates from rooftops, and a new phase of life is recognized. Resolutions are plentiful, yet with each passing day, dwindle into nothing more than insignificant memories of good intentions. Perhaps our shift in consciousness from an annual cycle of celebration may be refined to one where each day is embraced as a new life and rebirth – when each sunrise is experienced as the dawn of awakening compassion, altruism, and consciousness – within our own being; a daily moment when each sunset is a cleansing – a purging of fear, guilt, shame, and delusion – the end of hatred, indifference, and suffering.

I have every day to remind myself, if I choose – to celebrate today as a new beginning. I have this entire beautiful day to be alive on earth, among astronomical numbers of galaxies and unfathomable surplus of stars, suns, and planets – in the ever expanding cosmos.

I am honored to be awakening...becoming awareness on our mutually shared planet, which of course, includes: nature, my fellow humans, and all life. I am further honored by the infinite potential each one of us has to spend our day making conscious decisions and taking conscious action; or, to simply be.

In light of this amazing anomaly, 'life' – which is our shared collectively reality, we may choose to focus on one basic question: Tonight, when I lay my head down on my pillow, am I going to say to myself that I lived this year fully...for others...or...for myself...or...for all?

Billions of years ago, I was given the gift of consciousness by either a multitude of simultaneous random occurrences uniting at a single moment in time, or a higher intelligence (of some sort) joining with our scientific laws of the universe to spark life; probably a concerted effort of the two, yet, a humbling truth we will never know.

However, regardless of how or why I exist, what I do know is this: I AM here. And, how I choose to spend my day is ultimately, 'MY decision.' And, what I do...DOES affect others and our world. In order to alleviate my fears of insecurity, I can attempt to eliminate my worries by jumping into the rat race of making money; which is an egoic tactic resulting from feelings of unworthiness – of not being the 'right kind of provider' that society has programmed me to be.

I can also choose to become lost in the world of illusion by obsessing about all of the nice 'things' I can purchase for myself and children – that give me a false sense of purpose and self worth. I could even entertain my fictional motivation that was birthed from indoctrinated delusions of a higher being – a being that is going to make things 'all better' no matter what I do, and who removes 'all accountability' off of our collective responsibilities.

Am I choosing to forget about the reality of the cause and effect nature of everything: How our thoughts mold our behaviors, which, in turn, create the external world? And practically speaking, am I choosing to forget how the actions I perform 'on the job' may be ultimately contributing to the maladaptive normalcy of society, which embraces 'greed' and 'separation' – versus cultivating 'selflessness' and 'unity?'

Perhaps, I may simply choose to disregard this entire message I am reading right now, and continue my same patterns – to put off what I could be doing right now, until next year, in the form of a New Year's Resolution?

Am I turning a blind eye to my personal responsibility of what it really means to be human – to cultivate self compassion, generosity, and altruistic awareness, TODAY – this day? To inspire others, and "Be the change I wish to see in the world," NOW?

Having undeniable awareness that we live in an interdependent world, where truth is: change only occurs in the present moment of now, and all humans need each other in order to survive, do I possess the intense courage (and self compassion) to humbly ask myself the following: How am I part of the problem, and how am I part of the solution? Maybe, is it possible, that both our problems and solutions, are merely illusions.

Hmm…In the midst of this collective reality, maybe my New Year's Resolution may be asking myself these question…or…maybe…it will be my New Day's Resolution?

You Are Already That Which You are Seeking

To fit in, have needs met, and merely survive in physical form is what ego is designed for. Ego strives seeking options in order to create or sustain identities which have nothing to do with unconditional love. Please see that all identities are only possible as conditional survival mechanisms. Unconditional love and compassion can never be attributes of an identity. If one (an identity) seeks proof and reason to prove love and compassion exist, then the one seeking is not you – it is an identity – an illusion of self.

Love and compassion exist beyond reason, concept, thought, and form. Proving that love and compassion exist is like a droplet of water in the ocean trying to prove to other droplets that it is wet. Why would a droplet try to prove it is wet when it is wet? It must be the droplet's identity which has it seeking proof and validation; because, if the droplet could consciously see that it is wet, then the search would be over. Searching feeds suffering – giving it energy to sustain itself.

Why would one seek evidence of love when the very nature of the one seeking is love? End your search – look inward. Watch the one seeking. Percieve the one seeking.

Once more, you are already that which you are seeking. Can the one seeking be percieved?

A Glimpse of Passion

Isn't it amazing to feel so much intensity from within that it is nearly impossible to maintain an even breath, keep your nose from itching, or your eyes from tearing? Emotions so powerful that waves of memories rush back flooding your heart then depart so abruptly, leaving you gasping nothing more than, "Wow!?" Do you still try hard to remember the first perfect memory incessantly pondering until you reach its birth…when was yours?

Perhaps your first memory was when the world was a peaceful place? A moment in fictional time when innocence was virtuous and life didn't need to make sense? Was it a kiss or when you noticed your first love across the school yard? Maybe it was a bittersweet thought of a kindergarten crush offering their snack to some other lucky soul during a time when hearts raced and hearts were broken. Was it a time when all hope was lost?

But then! Out of nowhere stood someone glorious, yet seen so briefly, like a shooting star whose magnificence can only be seen just once. However short-lived, is it an image forever etched in falable memory or your deepest essence, whose dominance leaves you breathless and pondering, "Why?"

Why do we feel such deep emotions? We can't seem to put our finger on the exact cause. Does it start when the eyes see a physical entity so overwhelmingly breathtaking that all consciousness is abandoned and impulses override?

Do these thoughts occur at a level much deeper than our physical universe? A universe so obvious and present that it is unknowingly overlooked, leaving mind to construct fictional whims of individuality and unique emotions – felt during such a brief period – masking our true nature?

Maybe that connection and feeling of oneness isn't mind or emotion. Perhaps, there are two types of feelings: describable emotional feelings and indescribable feelings of grace.

Everything seems so fleeting. A period of time so brief, so tiny in length, that it can not be explained with ink and quill or even on canvas? How do we possibly describe such an intangibly personal experience felt only in our mind or is it the heart...or both? We could poetically describe this instance as a splinter in time or a fragment of a unique moment. Perhaps we could more appropriately honor this experience by deeming it "A Glimpse of Passion." Is this passion a doorway to the infinite that lives within?

I remember my adolescent glimpse vividly. However, I cannot feel the passion, that once perceived, overwhelmed my soul. It has faded like a castle in the sand that slowly diminishes with every heart broken wave. But then it happened in the midst of my journey…I was wandering through a desert of misery with the hypocritical sun beating down on my cloak of shame with infinite grains of torturous sand paving my path of uncertainty. I envisioned an oasis of calm, clarity, and from it arose a god.

It was a god of an ideal world that I selfishly imagined who had a magnificent vision to construct something perfect. I instantly decided to grant myself the power to create this being. I did it for no other reason than to restore my childhood fantasies, hopes, and dreams that once filled my heart but have long since vanished. As if this god were saying to me, "You never had to worry little one – it will happen and you will know."

But, then I realized I was just fooling myself once again. My imagination was playing games – egoic games of delusion once more. I knew then that the glimpse of passion was my humanness striving to be seen, felt, and heard – to quell physical angst – but it was not me; for I AM awareness…the awareness of imagination, the observer of emotion, the noticer of thought, in truth, the watcher of passion.

We Are All Here

O' how I long for the dearest part of me to come home. O' how guilt and shame drip from my pores during this spiritual journey called life.

Shame from knowing better yet action be hindered by perceived pain, loneliness, and fear.

Longing for the time when transcended dimensions prevail. Longing for the perpetual moment when humanity meets divinity.

There and only there my brothers and sisters will we be together.
One continuous moment captured by all who feel the union of love, presence.

I am here for you and you are here for me – we are one – we all belong.

We are all here.

Accepting Reality

If I cut off my arm and bury it in the dirt will it live forever? Am I, me, or my mind part of this body? Will my arm live forever beyond the mere physical components that made it a functional part of my human form? If I do the same to my leg, my other arm, my hair, my ears, my nose – will it affect me the same?

Am I so arrogant to think part of my soul dies with the death of a body part? Am I so conceited to think I even have a soul to begin with… …forgetting the soul is the soul itself? Or, am I courageous or ignorant enough to accept humans invented that confusing idea in the first place?

Will these thoughts empower me to see that my brain is nothing more than merely a body part which generates thoughts and perceptions of who I am – nothing more than an organ blocking me from witnessing life…distorting truth with mind-made meaning?

When my arm or leg or brain is no longer part of my body will I let it go and accept what it truly was – nothing but physical elements interdependently bonding with wonders of chemistry and biology, mutually joining forces to benefit my human experience? Or, will I wallow in shame of being less than a perceived person – pining for the lost part of me – yearning for deliverance from my suffering – craving for the story of immortality?

Perhaps relinquishing all attachments and delusions will thrust me into a higher state of being where I no longer fear 'what is'…to see with immense clarity and vivid understanding – not questioning 'what is' and letting go of 'what is not' as the only pathway to truth.

If it's not Joy - It's not me.
Direct your attention inward while reading this allowed to yourself.

If it's not joy – it's not me.
If it's not humility – it's not me.
If it's not compassion – it's not me.
If it's not love and peace – it's not me.
If it's not grace – it's not me.
If it feels separate – it's not me.

This One must let go of belief in joy – to realize this one's true nature – infinite joy.

This One must let go of belief in humility – to realize this one's true nature – infinite humility.

This One must let go of belief in compassion – to realize this one's true nature – infinite compassion.

This One must let go of belief in love – to realize this one's true nature – infinite love.

This One must let go of belief in peace – to realize this one's true nature – infinite peace.

This One must let go of belief in grace – to realize this one's true nature – infinite grace.

If it's judgment – it's not me.
If it's comparing – it's not me.
If it's analyzing – it's not me.
If it's doubting – it's not me.
If it's hating – it's not me.

If it's a feeling or thought of separation – it's not me.
If it's a feeling or thought of loneliness – it's not me.
If it's a feeling or thought of isolation – it's not me.
If it's a feeling or thought of abandonment – it's not me.
If it's shame – it's not me.

This One must let go of belief in need to judge – to realize this one's true nature – absence of judgment.
This One must let go of belief in need for comparing – to realize this one's true nature – absence of comparing.
This One must let go of belief in need for analyzing – to realize this one's true nature – absence of analyzing.
This One must let go of belief in need to doubt – to realize this one's true nature – absence of doubt.
This One must let go of belief in need to hate – to realize this one's true nature – absence of hate.

This One must let go of belief in thought of separation – to realize this one's true nature – absence of separation.

This One must let go of belief in thought of loneliness – to realize this one's true nature – absence of loneliness.
This One must let go of belief in thought of isolation – to realize this one's true nature – absence of isolation.
This One must let go of belief in thought of abandonment – to realize this one's true nature – absence of abandonment.
This One must let go of belief in shame – to realize this one's true nature – absence of shame.

If it's looking to past – it's not me.
If it's looking to future – it's not me.
If it's urgent – it's not me.
If it's anticipating – it's not me.
If it's afraid – it's not me.
If it's worry – it's not me

This One must let go of belief in need for past – to realize this one's true nature – indescribable here-now.
This One must let go of belief in need for future – to realize this one's true nature – indescribable presence.
This One must let go of belief in need for urgency – to realize this one's true nature – indescribable stillness.
This One must let go of belief in need for anticipating – to realize this one's true nature – indescribable peace.
This One must let go of belief in need

for fear – to realize this one's true
nature – indescribable unshakeable calm.

This One must let go of belief in need for
worry – to realize this one's true
nature – indescribable absence of worry.

If it's thinking – it's not me.
If it's doing – it's not me.
If it's suffering – it's not me.

This One must let go of belief in need for thinking – to
realize this one's true nature – watching the thinking.
This One must let go of belief in need for doing – to
realize this one's true nature – watching the doing.
This One must let go of belief in need for suffering – to
realize this one's true nature – incapable of suffering.

If it's physical – it's not me.
If it's a thought – it's not me.
If it's a feeling – it's not me.
If it's a memory – it's not me.
If it's a future projection – it's not me.
If it's a sensation – it's not me.
If it's an emotion – it's not me.
If it's mind – it's not me.

This One must let go of identification as (body) physical self – to realize this one's true nature.

This One must let go of identification as thoughts – to realize this one's true nature.

This One must let go of identification as feelings – to realize this one's true nature.

This One must let go of identification as memory – to realize this one's true nature.

This One must let go of identification as future projections – to realize this one's true nature.

This One must let go of identification as sensations – to realize this one's true nature.

This One must let go of identification as emotions – to realize this one's true nature.

This One must let go of identification as mind – to realize this one's true nature.

If it's resistance – it's not me.
This One must let go of resistance – to realize this one's true nature – infinite allowing.

If it's effort – it's not me.
This One must let go of effort – to realize this one's true nature – effortlessness.

If it's impermanent – it's not me.

This One must let go of belief and concept
of impermanence – to realize this one's
true nature – consciousness permanence.

If it's not here now – it's not me.
It it's not one with all that is – it's not me.

Watch the one who is letting go – this is you – the watcher. Watch the one who resists letting go – this is you – the one watching the resisting.

Embodiment of Grace

To be truly and honestly grateful at the highest level of consciousness, I must let go of everything I think is permanent, my illusion of happiness, and all I cling to for control and security.

The option to let go is only available now; and, once this purification is complete, I realize my true nature: the changeless pinnacle of graciousness, joy, and appreciation for life itself – as itself.

Meeting the bittersweet certainty of physical and mental death, and how this awareness provides abundant clarity to what it means to simply 'just be alive' – as the embodiment of grace.

Conditioned or Conscious Courage

Conditioned Courage is primarily unconscious and understood as 'the overcoming' of one's personal fears; fears propagated by many years of relentless unconscious programming and indoctrinated habitual patterns embedded by society, parents, and our own delusional thinking. To embrace and illicit conditioned courage is highly commendable, and indeed, a triumph over some of our deepest inner torment and angst – while reclaiming autonomy and individuality during that seemingly unavoidable, yet temporary, phase of human development.

True unconditional conscious courage, however, is absolute honest vulnerability as uncontested awareness, knowing that in the grand scheme of the universe – the ultimate cosmic game – that we weild absolutely no control over anything and everything, meaning: all we do in life is categorically insignificant; and, any manifestations that unfold on planet earth ultimately mean nothing, and the extinction of the entire human race in reality, is inevitable, thanks to the law of impermanence; all of which means: your life as you are currently perceiving it will eventually cease to exist, if not tomorrow, then one day. At a time unbeknownst to anyone; every single one of us will eventually die. Isn't this beautiful? Why not? Does your illusory self image feel jeopardized? Is your story of immortality blocking the truth that no one really dies – except in mind and body? Are your actions motivated by unconscious courage of mind or inspired by conscious courage of heart?

One becomes true conscious courage by persisting effortlessly with every formless ounce of their being – to rise above millions of years of selfish instinctual and mind-made impulses…impulses that reinforce personal survival and greed. The consciously courageous are unmoved by fictional accounts of omniscient supreme beings and remain unchanged by stories of immortality. Conscious courage lives free of grasping with one ultimate purpose: to let go of purpose, hence revealing purposeless grace within – thus cultivating the highest human potential which is always available now. And, when purpose dissolves, then unconditional love is revealed, and your homecoming is witnessed unto yourself – within.

Yet, the word homecoming is misleading since true consciousness, your boundless nature, has never left home dwelling in your heart and always accessible now. Your truest essence has merely gone unnoticed. Are you willing to take a courageous look inward – until you see that courage is not who you are? For that which you are, in truth, is grace and grace needs nothing – no courage at all to see.

My Human Friends

Finding human friends in a delusional world of unconscious minds, may at times, feel like locating and grasping a specific grain of sand among trillions resting at the bottom of the deepest ocean. It is not unfathomable, yet seemingly impossible – if you are blind.

Discovering mutual trust within another may take an extraordinary cascade of events leading to the awakening of our own highest and finest human self within - first. A process of awakening we must individually embrace and cultivate consciously within ourselves, before we can see the wonderful resounding oneness of humanity in others.

A profound meaning of a 'human friend' that comes to mind is: feeling a connection of such magnitude with another person that even the most exaggerated fiction conceivable pales in comparison; meaning: the connection is not imagined. This is someone that with a single glance into their eyes you feel warmth, understood, and connected beyond romance and emotion, and life simultaneously resonates meaning. This is the moment when you witness humanity (or is it divinity – truth), a divine human friend;

because you can see yourself in them.

Undeniably, we are ALL one of these people. Do you have the vulnerability to be a true human friend to another? Do you have the compassion to be a true human friend as yourself – to yourself, first – beyond duality of mind?

The human condition and ego often leave us perplexed and insecure about our physical appearance, stature, financial position, or who we are; most of the time we feel inferior or unworthy. In other words, many of us, (bound by our illusory self), are afraid of people and this false self, and don't even know it.

However, there is light! There are those in the world whose inner beauty and higher self have empowered them to see beyond the illusory covering (the physical body) and fictional accounts of self worth. Every waking moment they recognize the marvelous purity in others who cannot see it in themselves. I consider people like this to be magnificent creatures of life, love, and compassion.

Must I remind you, again, that you are one of these people? When you choose to see beyond your illusive identities of self preservation and perceived value, you will begin to notice that (you are truly) one of these individuals. The wonderful reality that you even wield infinite loving potential makes the world a better place! We are all lucky to have you…we are all very lucky to have each other.

My dear ones, let me share the following: Being a human friend does not require a sense of mutual participation from another and is not a two way street, requires no trust or conditions. Loving friendliness is relentless wisdom knowing I have a choice regardless of any unruly personal circumstance or global ill content running amuck in my mind. My purest nature (as does everyones') offers full awareness that I consciously decide to be a friend to whomever, whenever, no matter how they feel about me – even if I have never met them.

When I choose to cultivate loving thoughts or be genuinely kind to another, it comes with no strings attached and no expectation of reciprocation. Is this asking too much? Perhaps this seems impossible to you; maybe we could use some encouragement.

If you only remember one thing: everyday and especially during your most distraught times of angst, when the emotional woes of life are knocking at your door, a bad attitude has you in its grasp, or you feel like you are unable to be a friend to anyone, especially yourself, take a moment and look around. There are people among us who are speaking the following words (under their breath) when they see you, even if you do not notice:

"We are all in this together. My life instantly becomes happier because of you. Thank you so very much for this gift and for being one of my human friends mutually walking the Earth."

No Reason

Gratitude needs no reason.
Joy needs no reason.
Love needs no reason.
Humility needs no reason.
Compassion needs no reason.
Grace needs no reason.
Life needs no reason.
Presence needs no reason.
Truth needs no reason.

What you really are...
...needs no reason.

Open Your Eyes Now

Imagine living...and never becoming aware of unconscious mind programs running your life by ego. Imagine you finally reach the time when death is imminent, and find yourself inevitably pondering all the decisions you have made in life...? An epiphany occurs! Then, you realize almost everything you have been thinking and doing, over the course of your existence, has been primarily unconscious. You begin to experience the waking up process, which in part means: becoming aware of your unconscious motivations.

You reflect on all of the moments when purchasing things, manipulating others, and maintaining superficial relationships made you feel temporarily better. More clarity arises when you reflect on countless hours of mindless entertainment you experienced – which happened to place an impermanent smile on your face. As certainty of death grips you, your mind starts yearning for something, someone, or some thought, to quell the emotional pain, but to no avail, nothing can help.

You look around the room at all of 'those things' you have purchased and the comfort they once offered dissolves, with every glance. You reminisce about your bank account and the security your money once lent you, but it does not work anymore – money cannot help you now.

Yet another clarity arises when you scream out for god…the story of god you bought into from years of religious programming and myth. For the first time, however, you drop these mythical stories of hope, faith, and god and realize, 'There is no such thing.' You begin sobbing in truth NOT from sadness but from the relief that you now know there is something greater – truer than religious beliefs, ideologies, and fables.

You are further thrust into consciousness while unconscious beliefs continue to unravel. True awareness is brought forth illuminating your being with this fact: you just spent the only life you will ever have, basing your self-worth and happiness on fleeting conditions and things, money, delusion, and stature – surrounded by people just like you. You have allowed your ego to rule your life, unconsciously.

Tears begin to stream from your eyes because for the first time, ever, you have felt your higher self – authentic awareness – your core being – the essence of grace within. And, with bittersweet feelings of joy, tainted with a scent of melancholy glee, you ask yourself, "Why did I wait until now to open my eyes?"

Shedding Layers of Delusion

Imagine going through life grasping at fleeting happiness of virtually everything: buying more stuff, seeking entertainment, partaking in unconscious conversations with friends, and eating, proving time and time again that perceived experiences of joy we felt, were, and are, nothing more than temporary, or in other words, impermanent.

Imagine coming to terms with the fact everything we do in life…'all the doing' is merely a means and effort to alleviate pain, seek pleasure, and avoid suffering. For a moment you pause and contemplate what "doing" really is… and…at that instant (if your ego permits) you have a brief glimpse that in order to understand what 'doing' is, there must be something else counter to its meaning.

In a blink of an eye, a streaming thought inspired from your deep consciousness arises. It was a single thought you were able to catch a glimpse of. Not that you saw exactly what it was, but you noticed the profound essence of the idea. After careful and persistent concentration to see the thought, you begin to witness its meaning for the first time in your life. You see the thought and can differentiate it from the other countless ones creating endless white noise in the mind; the art of discernment is born; you witness that this thought is the concept of "being" – the antithesis to "doing." Maybe being is neither a concept nor thought but truth revealing itself through mind.

You experience a glimpse of reality offering insight that true happiness is unconditional and not discovered in doing, not in achieving, not in aspiring, not in gaining, not in expecting, not in anticipating; not even in trying, but simply in being – being itself.

For an instant, you realize you do not need to get anywhere, do anything, or obtain something in order to find consistent happiness, inner peace, contentment, gratitude, and love. You see beyond a shadow of a doubt that illusion of conditional happiness manufactured by ego has been sold to itself and adopted by you – as a bill of goods whose commodity is doing and thinking…falseness as predictable and consistent as clouds in the sky. Of course, this glimmer of true inner peace is short lived since honest peace and authentic joy are completely counter intuitive to what your ego has you thinking; so thinking immediately masks truth, again.

Although we talk about ego as a thing, an object, defining 'it' as if 'it' were a person with a personality, perhaps the person you think you are, and your personality, is simply ego, not you. Has ego been convincing you since you were born that you are any number of things, which are not true, like: a human doing; a human in search of peace 'out there;' a human on a quest to find happiness in the external world seeking material things; a person who has to accomplish, be heard, be outspoken, etc.

An infinite amount of mind-made delusions are why inner peace is so difficult to obtain – because peace is not something one can obtain – it only needs to be revealed – from within – you are that. Our peace is covered by selves, personalities, and identities. Peace can only be revealed by shedding layers of illusion, the hardened shell around your heart.

Let go of the delusions of seeking happiness out there, and relinquishing the craving for identity. Seek inward beyond mind, intellect, and meaning, and there you are…you are 'here now' watching everything.

Look Inward

When life's hardships, fears, and profound losses appear to consume every aspect of our being, remain still – look inward – and watch what is temporary.

When familial, social, and global state of affairs surpass any form of reason and erupt with selfish delusion, remain still – turn inward – and observe whatever arises then dissipates.

When you feel as if there is nowhere to run, that hopelessness is like a relentless deluge flooding your mind, heart, and soul with negativity and loss, remain still – focus inward – and notice what is changing.

Do not be afraid. Take a compassionate, honest look, inward. Inward offers the truest reality of our being – peace from within. There, peace is encapsulated by unwavering love, unlimited humility, and infinite acceptance.

When we have the compassionate heartfelt courage to look inward, peace reveals itself within every cell of the body. We soon are aware peace was always there. It never left. Peace IS you. It was only masked.

Unrelenting calm is restored within, and radiates into hearts and souls of countless others.

My Ego, My Friend, Good Bye

Preface: Please take a moment and replace you, your, and us with me, I, or my when appropriate. This change in content as you read from the first person point of view is profound.

Ego is like a very large muscular fifth grade friend you made when you were small because bullies on the playground were harming you, everyday.

The hardships of life appear in various forms to all of us (feeling like bullies), and our friend (ego) our bodyguard (and mind-guard), came to our rescue. Time and time again, your friend your ego never flinched, never left you alone, (and is still there protecting you.)

Lovely, for whatever duration the adolescent bodyguard (and mind-guard) hung around, there does come a time when one must depart from ego, our illusory layers of protection, in order for suffering to end. In other words, you discover it is time to grow up and awaken.

This "breaking up" is a paramount challenge since we have become deeply bonded with our ego, thus identified with this protector – who wants to continue protecting; therefore, we unconsciously allow the protector to carry on doing its unconscious job; hence, sustaining our suffering, unbeknownst to us.

It is as if you needed your bodyguard in grade school but when you got to high school and made new friends, no one really liked your bodyguard. You discovered the angry nature of your bodyguard was becoming a hindrance to expanding your horizons and friendships. In truth, you have seen that your ego-guard is angry due to fear, and you no longer want to precipitate more fear in your own being; you must decide whether or not to let your protector (and friend) go.

There comes a time in everyone's life (and typically several times) when we are confronted with a decision, whether or not to depart from what was once your best friend, in order to free yourself from fear that continues to bind you.

And, as unconscious nature of unconsciousness would have it, i.e. not having awareness to what is controlling our lives, in order to create some space between our truest essence and ego, we may have to look inward with receptive silence and recite the following thank you note:

> *Thank you ego, my ego, my dear friend. Thank you for protecting me when I did not know*

what to do, think, say, act, or feel. Thank you for protecting me since the day I was born to this day. With deep appreciation and gratitude, thank you for getting me this far in life. I can see now that you are not me – not who I really am. I no longer need or want to identify with your protection. It is time to step aside my friend and dissolve, or merely vanish - be free. By freeing you I am freeing my being. I relinquish you from your heartfelt duties of protection through avoidance, addiction, and compulsive thinking. I am letting you go, now, once and for all. My fearful ego, my friend, I love you, but we must part ways. I am not fear. Good bye…you won't be missed.

The Gift of Life – Rejoice NOW!!!

Every day awaken as you are – as a greeter of this gift – the gift of life. Rejoice NOW! This is the victory already won! Awaken now to this triumph that many of us never know.

Once one realizes this truth, recognition that anything and everything as it is, whether it is perceived as good or bad, is seen as merely a cherry on the desert of life. New awareness empowers inner vision to see every one of life's circumstances as opportunities to grow in compassion, forgiveness, joy, and love; as witness to all things beyond mind.

As the eternal present moment emerges as timeless presence, and as fear and shame holding you back from realizing and noticing your inner nature each morning dissolves, your resistance to 'what is' vanishes, and discovery of truth reveals itself – unwavering inner peace.

Revelation of gratitude for life itself is rediscovered, embraced, and witnessed. Rejoice the gift of life! Rejoice NOW!!!

The Changeless
Meditative Self Inquiry

The act of meditative self inquiry is available to guide those inward, who are willing to look, in order to see truth within. Self inquiry is a compassionate pointing to look inside, in order to see truth within; a chance to transcend the physical realm by seeing through direct experience that which our true nature is – is formlessly existing as non-physical essence of changelessness – absolute awareness – pure grace – which is always available here now – as you; this indescribable intangible truth is the same location-less dimension that enlightened beings have been directing us towards, within, for millennia.

Have you had enough suffering in the physical mind-made world of illusions? Are you ready to take a look within? Are you ready to take an honest look within to rediscover your true nature – that which is changeless?

The best recommendation for this meditative self inquiry is to record the following from your own voice. This method allows you to become acquainted with your deepest consciousness (your inner guru as your truest nature) who is helping you awaken. Please note that these practices are NOT events in order to gain some semblance of peace after a rough day – like many mediation and yoga practices. Meditative self inquiry is a 'happening' to partake in – for you to experience, directly, your true nature. However, you may discover that a consequence of witnessing your inner most being is peace and stability.

You may need to partake in this happening many times. Typically, resistance will arise, which indicates you are getting close to seeing. Stay the course. Notice, there are three parts to this Meditative Self Inquiry. They are designed to flow together, so record all three in succession. However, if you want a shorter session, you may utilize only Part One as you begin introducing yourself to meditative self inquiry. As you record, please allow pauses, from seconds to minutes; whatever you feel in your heart seems agreeable.

Part One:

Please take a seat and close your eyes. Now drop all concepts of what you are doing right now. Drop all expectations; drop all ideas; drop all analysis. Drop the need and trying to figure things out. Drop all trying; drop all needing. Drop all future notions. Drop the idea of future. Now, also, drop the idea of past. Drop the idea of time, altogether. Dwell in timelessness. Drop memory. Drop everything. Let everything go. What is left?

Is what is left concerned with time? Does it hope? Does it worry? Is it troubled with the past, or future?

Let sensations go, drop them. Let feelings go, drop them. Let emotions go, drop them. Let the voices, go, drop them. What is left? Can you perceive-notice: sensations, feelings, voices, memories, and emotions? Whatever arises, can you notice it, perceive it? Whatever arises…is it changing – does it leave? If whatever arises is you, then when it leaves, wouldn't you be gone, too? But, you are still here – now.

Who is noticing and perceiving all that arises? Is what is noticed you, or are you the one who is noticing? Continue to sit in silence for 5 minutes marinating in this space.

Part Two:

When one says, "I must do this" or "I must do that" or "I am depressed" or "I am anxious," Who is 'I?' When you say 'I' – is that 'I' person noticed – watched – perceived? Is that 'I' really you…or an idea of you…or the real you – your true nature as pure awareness? In any of the above statements, if the 'I' is noticed by you, then must there be one that is noticing; we will call the one who is noticing, the noticer. Is the noticer, you?

Who is doing the noticing and perceiving of all things

internal and external? What about emotions, feelings, sensations, thoughts, and memories? Who notices and perceives all of that? If all mental noise, voices, and bodily sensations are noticed and perceived, then who is the one noticing and perceiving? Is that one, you? An idea of you? Can the one who is noticing, be noticed, perceived?

Who is the one interpreting the sensory data and information? Who is the one associating, labeling objects, and assigning meaning? Is that one, you? Is something present which sees that associating, labeling of objects, and assigning of meaning? Have you noticed that meaning changes over time? For example, the ideas we had about ourselves when we were ten years old were not the same ideas we had of ourselves when we were in our teens; then, 20's; then again in our 30's; and so on. All of your perceptions of yourself (and others) are constantly changing? Amidst all of the changing, what isn't changing? What is changeless?

On a moment to moment basis, memories are changing; thoughts arise then instantly fade away, and some thoughts may stay a little longer but eventually pass away; sensations come and go like clouds, emotions intensify like waves in the ocean, stay for a while then are gone the next minute, week, month, or year. But, all of them are impermanent. If you were literally thoughts, memories, sensations, feelings, and emotions, then when they go, then wouldn't you be gone too? But, here you are, right here now.

Have you noticed that absolutely everything is constantly changing – everything?

If nothing ever stays the same, then how could it be possible to hold onto anything, whether it brings happiness or sadness? If feelings, thoughts, emotions, sensations, and memories immediately or slowly fade away, always, then what is the benefit of holding onto any of them? Why not drop them, now? Or, not even become attached to them in the first place? What is underneath all of that changing? Who is there witnessing all of the constant changing? Does the one 'witnessing the changing,' ever change? Does it have opinions? Does it care about time? Does it have hopes…dreams?

Is it possible, that underneath the conditional psychological spectrum of emotions, with shame at one end of the spectrum and happiness at the other, that there is the capacity to experience unconditional joy and peace, now, beyond the ups and downs of conditional emotions and feelings? Underneath all of the body and mind noise, are you the silent joyous, peaceful truth underneath all of the mind noise…a silent witness – which does not change? Is it possible that your deepest, truest essence, you, is changeless?

See for yourself…what does not change? While everything external, and your physical body, and mental noise is in a constant flux, what stays the same? Be honest. Allow yourself to be honest, here now – to your true nature. Everything is constantly changing except one thing…awareness; unbiased, pure, awareness – as grace itself – you. What if part of our block is that we view change as something that happens then is over, instead of a more honest approach, which is this: some 'things' don't change – everything IS changing – constantly. Change is NOT an event.

Things don't change in the future – the future has never existed – things are already changing, now, out of our awareness. People don't change in the future – the future has never existed – they are already perpetually changing, now, out of our awareness. Places don't change in the future – the future has never existed – places too, are already constantly changing, now, out of our awareness. Our belief systems are continually changing; and, our beliefs and ideas about ourselves are always in a state of flux, as well, right now, out of our awareness. Who we think we are is constantly changing, and so on, and so on it goes. Are you aware of what is changing within? Have you noticed and observed those changes – the changing? Are you the awareness of what is changing – the perceiver of changing? Are you that which is changeless? Is it possible you are nothing more than unbiased pure formless awareness…pure essence as unconditional love?

Has your perception of you ever "changed" or is it constantly changing? Did you notice the change in your perceived self? Is that perceived self really you? Who (in your own being) noticed the change? If you noticed a change in yourself, then who is the one who noticed? The one who changed or something else, or both? What became aware of that change in your perceived self? Awareness? Continue to sit in silence and marinate in stillness for a little while.

Part Three:

What causes a great deal of suffering is 'wanting' to hold onto things that are constantly changing; for instance, holding onto the idea of who we think we are. Most everyone is perplexed about who they are – not sure where or how they fit into life – which causes a great deal of worry, anxiousness, anger, and depression. Is that suffering coming from the perceived self or something deeper? Please note: all suffering is at the level of mind, not absolute awareness; suffering does not come from your true nature.

We struggle to maintain the illusion of control through mind, believing that things only change on occasion, and believe the ideas we have about ourselves are permanent (not true). Ego-mind wants us to hold onto something which is fleeting – illusory ideas of our selves which are constantly changing. If someone tries to balance a marble on the tip of a toothpick which is constantly moving, what will result? How does one hold onto the idea of who they are – when that idea is constantly shifting and moving – without becoming frustrated, angry, or unconscious? Mind does not want our true nature to see the perceived personae, identities, and ideas of our selves, because they will dissolve when the light of awareness is shined on them.

We, therefore, become scared and angry when we notice the changing, especially when we try to break free from our normal patterns; as if this change was a surprise. If one lives in denial to this reality, that all things are changing (the law of impermanence), then how could that being ever be truly happy, permanently, unconditionally? Virtually every person on the planet has been conditioned and trained that permanent joy and peace does not exist, (which is not true). Most people are so deeply used to suffering as part of existence that they don't even give conscious awakening a chance – a possibility to have suffering end altogether – to see their core being – underneath mind and body – to discover or re-discover their true nature – unbiased peace and joy as graceful awareness watching the play of life.

Please listen with an open mind and open heart: Our true nature is pure awareness, as non-physical grace, as formless stillness, before any conditioning, before mind-made ideas and concepts, before emotions, thoughts, intellect, memories, feelings, and sensations. The understanding of our deepest essence does not come in the form of verbal or intellectual answers – only through direct indescribable experience, within.

However, since birth, we have been conditioned to exist only in the physical realm of existence (pure survival), which is not truth of existence. In other words, we have become so deeply identified with body and mind that we project these physical beliefs on the external world – so everyone continues validating each other's unconscious conditionally physical reasons to suffer; which is why physical beauty, fancy cars, and intellect are greatly admired and also cause great suffering; they are all physical attributes which tell nothing about the essence of one's inner being. Those things are all ego stuff which do nothing to help one liberate one's self – to discover inner freedom – to experience true formless freedom within. Continue to sit in silence and marinate in being for a little while.

Your Answers are Within
Contemplation Meditation

When a Master speaks of grace, compassion, love, humility, and honor, and says, "You are that." the mind immediately begins asking: "What is grace? What is compassion? What is love? What is humility? What is honor?" Mind is seeking an answer to these questions so mind can have oppressive rules to live by. Mind wants your true self to adopt rules and beliefs in mind processes and concepts, in order to keep you lost in an endless gerbil wheel of searching; hence, leading you on a wild goose chase away from truth.

All monkey mind obsessing and searching are temporarily designed to distract you from knowing for yourself – within yourself – that you are the embodiment of grace, love, compassion, and humility, already; and, no search for yourself is necessary – for you are always here now. You are indescribable love itself, yet mind distracts your attention from knowing that which you already are.

For example, mind typically defines love as someone who does good things, then mind develops a persona or identity of one who does good things. This way, the mind can then validate itself by believing you are a good person by saying, "See look at me, I am loving because I do good deeds and help people." The mind continually tries to define everything; and more intensely when on a spiritual quest. If doing good deeds makes you a good and loving person, then you would only have to do one good deed, and you are done, right? But, in order to be a good person, mind has us stuck in a merry-go-round of suffering where we must continue doing good deeds for the remainder of our lives, in order to feel good about ourselves; this is an impossible request – which is a huge reason why we continue suffering.

Good deeds do not make a person good, in the same way, bad deeds do not make a person bad. A person is already the embodiment of goodness – before the perception of good or bad deeds ever happened – before you even took your first breath. Let's try this: Allow me to state "There is nothing wrong with you." Now say "There is nothing wrong with me" to your self and listen for mind who may disagree. (Pause here and spend a few moments or a week or as long as it takes contemplating the last few sentences.)

Much like trying to figure out the last few sentences, keeping you stuck in an idea that something is wrong with you, mind continues trying to define grace, compassion, love, humility, and honor, etc. so you become lost in obsessive thinking and learning how to behave, (in order to become a "good person.") Please see that mind wants to define everything; definitions are nothing more than veils masking truth which these words (grace, compassion, love, and humility) point to. The truth that these words are pointing to are NOT definable in terms of thoughts, concepts, more words, or behavior, and cannot be understood through language or communication. Before memory, ideas, thoughts, feelings, emotions, sensations, conditioning, and beliefs, YOU are love and grace and compassion and humility, beyond mind-made understanding. In that way, there is no need to define them. If the mind were to stop for a moment, hence removing thought and memory filters, you would instantly see what your true nature is – beyond description, concept, and definition...realization of your true nature...grace.

Here is a story. A Master looks out into the world and sees practically every human being on earth has covered their deepest essence with many layers of conditioning; i.e. I am this or that. In other words, and speaking in a mildly poetic sense: conditioning are veils of delusion we wear skewing our perception of truth; much like a hardened shell around our heart – blocking the most fundamental piece of life within us.

Moving on with the story, one of the many unconscious beings on earth comes to the Master as a student and says,

"Master, please guide me. I am willing to see the truth, now."

The Master replies, "You are already that which you are seeking."

The student asks, "Then, what am I so I will know."

The Master humbly states, "Because your mind has already assigned meaning to words, please see that everything I say to you will be misunderstood. These words are only pointers to truth, but not truth itself. What you already are, in truth, is indefinable and can only be experienced within."

The student answers, "Yes Master. But, what am I?"

The Master replies, "You are compassion, grace, love, and humility…stillness."

The student says, "Thank you Master. I feel this at times, but what is compassion, grace, love, and humility?"

(Can you see the gerbil wheel spinning in the dialog above? No matter what the Master says, the mind has another question. See if you can catch your own mind doing that.)

Here's an analogy: The student in the story is like a person whose skin has been painted blue with several coats. But, since these layers of paint began covering the student, the moment he or she left his or her mother's womb as an infant, then the person has no idea their blue colored skin is really not him or her true color. In a way, the student simply doesn't know any better. Much like the example above, the student is not aware the mind is asking these questions, not the student's true nature. (SEE HERE NOW if you can catch your mind asking, what is true nature?) Note that the paint in this analogy is conditioning, and every human being is subjected to conditioning immediately following birth – which continues piling on for the totality of everyone's life. (Until we begin to awaken, that is.) You see, we think we are the conditioning; conditioning as concepts, stories, ideas of 'I' – false belief systems of who you are – 'who I am.'

In a way, (but mostly in truth), the student has never seen himself or herself without the paint (conditioning), or the student wouldn't have to ask the Master anything. People simply accept the paint as who they are (a blue person), and continue through life never seeing or consciously questioning what is really there underneath the layers of conditioning. What exists underneath conditioning is pure still essence of life – YOU – the watcher.

Moreover, when the student, in the story above, asks for definitions of grace, love, compassion, and humility, the problem is with every definition heard, another layer of paint is added to his or her skin since mind is constantly trying to 'figure out' and assign meaning to everything, seemingly begetting only more questions from the student. Some aspect of mind is always the one asking, not the students true nature. (Note that the student's true nature would never ask what 'it' is – because 'it' already knows.)

So, if you are already painted with many layers of blue paint since birth, and you look in the mirror to see who you are, then you see 'blue' a normal person. Which means, if you add a few more layers of blue paint (more content), in the form of definitions that you misinterpret, offered by your Master's pointings, or a book, or video or workshop, and look in the mirror again, what will you see? (Pause and ask yourself this before reading ahead.)

The answer is, "more blue paint" but not the deepest truth of you. You will see yourself as you have always seen yourself, a blue person (with more blue paint) who does not know that the blue layers are NOT you, because you are seeing yourself through the blue memory filter of mind. (Note: All spiritual masters are using content as tools to help us look below the conditioning – not add more blue paint.) So, by adding a few more layers of blue paint, what will happen to your perception of you? Pretty much nothing, except by adding more layers typically means more confusion you will have to muddle through later on. So… what do you think…should you continue adding more layers? Or, stop allowing mind to use content as paint instead of tools to sincerely look inward.

Sometimes a person will catch a glimpse of truth when a Master says, "You are already that which you are seeking." and their perception is shifted slightly. They look in the mirror and see a blue person, but this time it is different, because they have a suspicion that what they are seeing (now) is NOT 'who I think I am.' This means that the words are beginning to be discovered with something other than their ears – the opening of the heart. One must become open and soften or the answers will cover you in more blue paint. One must listen with the seed of truth within – underneath the blue paint – beyond mind – beyond words – beyond concept. So, how does one avoid adding more blue paint?

One answer is to recognize that you are currently seeking answers outside of yourself. One more possibility is to limit the content you put into your head and sit in receptive silence more often with a phrase or paragraph that resonates with your core being. For example, you hear a short talk on a video that really hits home; listen to it over and over; consistently sit with it in loving contemplative openness. In other words, listen with your heart, not your head.

Please be aware: one ego trap can be when a person becomes addicted to spiritual knowledge and gets caught in the gerbil wheel of content. This person typically continues buying book after book, attending countless self help meetings, or going to one retreat or workshop after another, but yet, has not been able to surrender the fact that the answers they are seeking are within. That same person, if they had accepted their answers are within, would immediately find him or herself not wanting to add more content to the mind, but in fact, limit the content.

The ego likes to play the positive feedback game, too. This occurs when a little pearl you find in a book gives you a short feeling of relief (not the happiness you are seeking), THEN when that feeling wears off, you buy another book so you can get that feeling back – get another 'fix.' All the while, you are no closer to truth and no more happy; perhaps, more frustrated. This chasing of the tale can happen in a variety of ways because, what is inside can be very scary to see and address honestly and consciously, and it is easier to get lost in external content – searching externally.

Moving on, one fundamental aspect of truth spoken by every enlightened being is some version of the following: "Stillness is your true nature." If you ask what this means then you are typically adding more layers to yourself – unless you are really listening with your heart – the seed of truth within – the one who does not question but is silently watching the questioner. This is why the ultimate advice any Master can offer is silence and stillness. Just sit there and allow calmness and quietness to arise while you observe your mind thinking and questioning and remembering. That, is looking inward. However, words must be spoken in order to help break through layers of resistance, and point and guide those genuinely ready to watch their suffering end. Let us not get lost in trying to 'figure out' meaning with mind, but allow openness to reveal what these words are pointing to.

So, "If you are already that which you are seeking," which is the context of life (stillness) underneath the content (data), and more content is continually being added in the form of information and definitions, then how will you ever see your true nature? (Please pause and contemplate this question.)

One way of answering the question is to begin or continue listening with your heart...the truth within, underneath the words. Due to layers of paint (conditioning) and illusory self images, listening with one's heart does not readily present itself. Most of the time, we must begin utilizing various techniques to let go of stuck emotional energy and feelings. I highly recommend beginning with grieving and forgiveness. Talking to someone whom you trust about forgiveness, and grieving with them can be very beneficial, and typically must happen before true heart opening occurs. In other words, getting out what we have suppressed, oppressed, depressed, and repressed, allows our hearts to soften.

Please understand, in the traditional form of grief, in my experience, we grieve until we see that we no longer must grieve; because the final detachment to the thought form causing grief is a letting go process – which is a choice. Note that, in truth, what actually does the grieving is not your true nature, not you, but a component of ego or ego itself – a mind construct. Authentic grieving appears to always be a letting go of something which you are not.

Dissolving initial layers of resistance are very important to the spiritual process. There are a certain amount of layers that seemingly must break down before one is wholeheartedly willing to see, the answers you really are seeking really are within.

Once enough layers of resistance dissolve, then potential for fully committing to spiritual awakening will happen, effortlessly.

Beyond the Veil of Vanity

How do you tell a woman she is beautiful without stroking her ego, hence, reinforcing culture's unconscious delusions of beauty and self worth?

Looks do not last yet we attempt to capture them with pictures, that when relived, offer nothing but another brick in the mortar of personal and collective suffering, where: wishes for youthful appearance, attempts to compare the past to the wrinkled now, and memories of a firm body are nothing more than distractions to what really matters – inner beauty.

With every stroke of the makeup brush, every pat of powder, accentuated coloring, illusion of lifted cheeks, smooth forehead, lips, and so forth, I wonder, "Who are you trying to cover up? What are you dissatisfied with? When will you get tired of the charade? Where will the next delusional inadequacy surface? Why all the trouble? Who are you trying to impress? How does this make a person happy?" (How are men doing the same thing? Anyone?)

How do you honestly share with a woman that her rear-end 'looks great!' when you do not even notice her back side – because your addiction to appearance is dissolving?

How do you sincerely put into words that her breasts, hair or legs are 'perfect' when you see beyond them – because your perceptions are no longer influenced by societal conditioning or ego?

How do you genuinely compliment a woman on anything physical when the body part will have the exact same value in 50 years as it does today – because, in reality, looks do not matter?

So…how do you tell a woman she is beautiful beyond the veil of vanity? It may go something like this:

> *I see your compassionate and loving heart – your gentle nature. I see the real you – your appearance matters not. I see your unencumbered beauty – always have and always will – beyond the veil of vanity.*

You Are Wherever You Go

Changing geography in search of happiness is like using a blanket to shelter oneself from the rain. There is a brief moment of comfort, yet after a short period of time, the coldness and dampness will be felt, once again. And then...one yearns for another blanket.

Seeking geographical refuge from ones ego and suffering is impossible since ego is your shadow which follows you wherever you go – until your light of consciousness shines infinitely dispelling all darkness – regardless of physical location. And, what you really are, consciousness, never leaves...you are that.

No matter where you go, there you will be.

However, changing geography to set you in an environment more suitable for seeking inward, where there are those who resonate with deep understanding of stillness, silence, and truth, can be greatly beneficial to spiritual awakening.

Choose wisely.

Honoring Earth
The Bearer of Truth

O' Mother Earth…or…should I call you Father…or, simply Earth? Maybe it would be more honoring to call you, 'The God of Human Life;" I don't know…in fact…I know nothing…I don't know who you are, or if in deed, you are a you. A you with emotion? Empathy? Or simply another identity my imagination has conjured up by unconscious will of ego – distracting me from seeking 'truth' that already lives within.

Yes…that's it! I have found my words now, O' great essence of life giving substance and simultaneous taker of life…thank you…

…as I lay prostrate, submerged in an unknowing, I summon the tiniest most insignificant aspect of my mind in effort to put words into the air – to honor you, Earth. Thank you, O' essence of nature for demonstrating truths of existence; the truth that all life, both animate and inanimate, was birthed from an unknown intellectually creative life force that lives within you, and me; an unbiased life force that taught you to create unconditionally – with no boundaries – with no judgment – with no shame or guilt.

I honor you Earth, for teaching us absolute truth of existence – that nothing lasts – that nothing is permanent (except pure awareness). Thank you for showing us that conditional judgments we place on people, places, things, thoughts, and circumstances, are in reality, invented by us – only create conditions causing our own suffering.

Thank you for creating us in the fluid form of your beautiful face – the oceans – of which we have discovered our bodies to primarily consist of. I honor the unconditional life-giving gift of water that you bequeath to us, which is unknowingly discovered in the form of moisture when we leave the womb – when we are forced to exhale making space for yet another unseen aspect of your nature – air.

Dear Earth, I more emphatically honor you with a deep sense of humility, the unconditionality of your life-giving substance, water: On one hand offering life, yet on the other, taking it away by the power of your seas – ending tens of thousands of human and nonhuman lives while simultaneously allowing others to give birth.

I give thanks to your unconditional nature, which honors this absolute truth: That the essence or life force of existence: IS unbiased, IS unconditional, IS NOT prejudiced, doesn't laugh, and doesn't cry. You prove to me time and time again that you care NOT about race, color of skin or fur, species, religious beliefs, political agendas, sexual orientation, or any man-made, (rather, mind-made) labels we separate ourselves from you with.

When a tiny child drowns in your life-giving essence of life, it doesn't matter the color of his or her skin. When a one hundred foot wave destroys entire cities, you do not think about the race or nationality of those whom will soon perish. When your rains combine with the very life-blood of all creation (soil) sliding down mountains killing entire villages, you do not take inventory of the language they speak, or which god they pray to.

O' Earth, or whatever you are, that has provided this infinitesimal component of all that is, a single molecule of water, thank you for making all of your other essences available to us – to all life – which interdependently and simultaneously allow us to physically exist as timeless presence – until you unconditionally recycle our physical components back into you, at a time determined by neither you nor I – but by something greater.

In closing, allow me to honor that everywhere I turn, you offer me another sign of impermanence, a sign of truth: a colorfully changing leaf on a tree, a wrinkling face aging with gravity, the ever changing process of our food supply, a smile, a frown, the wind, the rain, my friends, my body, my thoughts – nothing stays the same.

When I look deep within your red heart using my imagi-

A LOVING INVITATION TO LOOK WITHIN

nation, your core, there is a force perpetually pulling us into you. Then, you repeatedly push all recycled matter out unto the surface, proving that everything is nature – all of us are nature. I am you and you are us. In this way, we never die, yet, in the exact same paradoxical way, we are constantly dying.

Wait…when I sequester my mind and simply be…this paradox dissolves and I am exposed to your unbiased nature – which many call unconditional love, which too, is my nature. You do not seem to care if I live or die…or…who I am…or…who I think I should be, or become – which is spectacular. You seem to merely be a process within a process, and us…a process within yours – where you are nurturing us to simply 'be,' while be-andering in physical form.

Your unconditional nature is wonderfilled; which appears to be the only 'truth' you CAN teach us, by example. The never-ending evidence and perpetual facts you place before our very eyes, which get lost in delusion - is beautiful – which very few of us have the courage to see or live. Your uncaring is beautiful; for with your uncaring you offer us, again, truth of impermanence:

Everything is changing and no one, not even you, has any control over it.

Thank you, O' bearer of truth…thank you, Earth…thank you.

You are the Difference

Money comes and goes like fading clouds.
Governments rise and fall like breaking tides.
Religions and cultures inevitably evolve and dissolve.
And thoughts, feelings, and
perceptions, change like the wind.

But truth lasts forever.

Make a profound impact on the world now, by seeking
inward, so your fellow human ancestors may live in peace.
Give not only of material, but of wisdom, action,
grace and love.

You are truth – you are life – you are the difference.

Acceptance and Egoic Games

Preface: The following piece has been written more from the perspective of mind, not necessarily enlightenment directionals pointing 'beyond mind;' henceforth, there is reference to 'changing thinking' in order to lesson suffering. Please know that all suffering is a result of being identified with thinking-mind. And, the only way to end suffering is to become completely dis-identified with body-mind; whereas, changing thinking may lesson suffering temporarily but never end it completely. However, having the awareness as described in the following piece can help you notice how autonomy of mind can help maintain control over your physical being.

In life we are faced with many individual and collective challenges, problems, and situations which bring us suffering. Typically, there are only three choices when addressing any of (what we consider) life's unfortunate circumstances. They are: change our thinking, accept the circumstances, or physically leave the situation. When we find ourselves in an unhappy state of affairs, many of us get caught in a mindset of wanting to change the situation in order to be happy. Often times, people fool themselves into thinking that (hoping for change) is actually change. They may find themselves in a marriage, job, country, or society where 5 to 10 to 20 years later nothing has changed – the drama is the same. The pain was simply masked and the only difference is they have fallen into a more unconscious state of self denial.

Another choice we have when things don't go our way is to accept or resist whatever perceived unhappy situation or life circumstance we currently are experiencing. Many people find "accepting" to be the only option when they ultimately discover no one can change another person but only themselves, and leaving seems too overwhelmingly painful.

However, a fundamental ego acceptance trick which may arise is that 'simply accepting' most often times maintains the exact dysfunctional environment and complacent relationships, employment, and culture, which may be counterproductive to spiritual wellbeing. This means you may unknowingly maintain or degrade your current process of awakening while reinforcing a false identity, which is to say, you will be incapable of changing your thinking to a more efficient manner of enhancing your inner clarity. Ego can also mask honest spiritual acceptance by taking on a new role of "if you can't beat them then join them." You may defy seeking help, new employment, or new relationships to help move you beyond your current complacent level of drama.

Unfortunately, by simply jumping on someone else's band wagon of ill content, one may be unconsciously enabling him or herself to believe they are happy, when in fact, they are only temporarily using egoic acceptance as a coping mechanism. For example, a person may put on the "game face" of happiness and project an image of happy when deep down, (if they are deeply honest with themselves), they are unhappy and simply fooling themselves – to avoid dealing with deeper issues; like the pain and hardened shell around their heart – a false identity. (Actually, all identities are false.)

The phrase "my best thinking has got me here" is a wonderful example when one finally realizes their identity is nothing more than decisions in life based upon conditional thought processes. Unless the core problem, which is distorted thinking is addressed, they will most likely end up in the same unhappy relationships, marriage, and jobs, where drama and dysfunctional environments, that were once accepted, becomes there self perpetuating cycle of demise.

Ultimately, to know our true nature is to become aware of thoughts – you are the awareness, the stillness that watches both dysfunction and beauty. However, we must gain some autonomy of our thoughts and actions using our mind in order to 'tame the ox', for now; hence, this piece of literature you are reading this moment.

Acceptance is a wonderful thing if acceptance is truly what you are doing. The pitfall is most individuals believe becoming complacent and accepting a particular level of dysfunction and drama is somehow noble – without having a plan to honestly seek and address root causes of suffering – at a conscious level – beyond identity.

In addition, ego often loves to masquerade as one who simply accepts everything and everyone regardless of who or what they are; some people may call you Jesus or the Buddah, thus a subtle egoic identity named 'the acceptor' is covertly working. Many people trick themselves into thinking passivity and full acceptance is enlightenment. Ego is clever and can use open acceptance as a means of projecting wishes and hopes for acceptance of itself – a false identity.

Please do not misinterpret what I am pointing at here; acceptance can be a wonderful tool for breaking maladaptive thought patterns to gain clarity while discovering your humanness; humanness as the manifested expression of what you really are, consciousness.

However, acceptance is usually a covert way for ego to gain personal acceptance as a projection and desire to be liked. The need to be liked is an illusory idea and why we continue trying to fit in, since we haven't realized there is nothing physically there which needs acceptance. All we truly are is an empty spaceless-space of timeless grace, compassion, and love.

Moreover, the ego (our survival system) may use 'accepting' as a coping mechanism to evade dealing with guilt, shame, and fear of not being accepted by others. Please know that all suffering is an illusion created by mind and sustained by an illusory identity. Most of us have adopted a false belief that we cannot accept our own self, 'yourself.' But, this is only more of the illusion. (In truth there is no finite mind-made identity (myself), yet we 'think' there is; we are lost in personhood instead of being as we are – in beingness.)

In truth, our truest nature can be described as effortless genuine appreciation of everyone, and everything, beyond acceptance.

Becoming aware of the difference of your shame driven need for personal acceptance and genuinely accepting others, typically requires a spiritual practice with some combination of the following: forgiveness, grieving, mediation, yoga, stillness, non manmade nature (trees, forest, rivers, lakes, open plains, etc.) and prolonged silence, and deeply honest self inquiry.

Discerning between personal conditional acceptance (suffering) and unconditional acceptance (our true nature) is a wonderful step in reaching consistent inner peace and realizing who you are not. What you really are is NOT an identity.

Truth – Knowing the Unknown

True consistent inner peace is a result of first, embracing the possibility of truth, which typcially means one must let go of illusory belief systems.
Truth is not about belief, not a belief, and not a belief system. Truth is not even about believing or disbelieving the words you are reading right now. Truth is not about believing one can save the world; is not about discovering the secrets of the universe either; and, is not saying that you know something then spending your entire life selling yourself and others on the idea.

Truth is more along the lines of not knowing. Truth is not about knowing information yet embracing fearlessness, wisdom, and humility to be open to the possibility of unknowing. Truth is closer to having absolute awareness, clarity, and certainty – that you will never know – the great "I don't know."

And, when you ultimately surrender to this reality with your entire being, then fear, guilt, and shame, as ego identification dissolve; and, resistance, as anxiety and depression, lose their stronghold, and ultimately exist no more. Your heart softens, inner peace never abandons, the struggle ends, and you finally start to live – all from surrendering to "I don't know."

Looking directly into the unknown with humility and compassion allows grace to effortlessly radiate within, as you witness life unfolding in the timeless present moment, as presence. When the last drop of resistance to the unknown evaporates from your mind, in a way, your higher self is reborn; truth is seen.

The Power of Belief

The Power of Belief is certainly becoming clear to many of us, and perhaps, completely understood as fundamental truth to those willingly awakening their consciousness. In other words, every person in the world was born with innate human ability to choose to believe whatever they want to believe – at any moment; evolution has wielded us with this power. (Assuming, you and I have made a decision to believe in evolution.) What do you choose to believe?

Speaking in first person as if you were talking to yourself, if I want to believe in Santa Clause, then I can choose to believe in Santa Clause. If I want to believe in the Easter Bunny, then I can choose to believe in the Easter Bunny. If I want to believe that the Earth is round versus flat, then I can choose to believe it. I can also believe that one plus one equals 2 or I can believe that one plus one equals 3 – it is my choice what I believe.

I have had many conversations with human beings who believe in ideas and concepts that many others believe to be completely fiction. I have also seen many cultures and subcultures who partake in what most of us would consider to be 'insane practices,' for spiritual reasons, like: worshiping cows, snake handling, talking to the dead, eating the body of Christ, and drinking blood, to name a few. Of course, when we are consciously honest with ourselves, most of us will admit we believe in something that could be perceived by someone else as an insane point of view; regardless if we identify as: Atheist, Agnostic, Christian, or what-have-you.

If I want to believe in one or all of the 33 million Hindu gods, then I can choose to believe in them. Conversely, if I want to believe that people who worship multiple gods are crazy, then I can. When something good happens in my life, I can thank 'Jesus' for it – assuming I have chosen to believe that 'Jesus' allowed me the courtesy. Or, perhaps, it's just dumb luck. If I win the lottery, say…ten million dollars, depending on my religious beliefs, I can choose to believe that 'Yahweh' blessed me with the money – that is, if I have made a decision to call myself Christian. If I choose to call myself Muslim, then I will most likely make a decision to thank Mohamed for this kindness – if I win the sweepstakes. If I believe I am a Western Buddhist, then I would probably thank the Buddha for my good fortune when the lottery commission announces, "You won!" However, if I am an Eastern Buddhist, then I would possibly chock the lottery up as 'good luck' or Karma. If I am Atheist, then I would potentially say it was nothing more than the theory of probability. What I decide to believe is categorically my choice, isn't it? Don't I get to choose to believe whatever I want? Whether it makes sense to others or not? Don't you? Doesn't every person on the planet have this ability and innate right?

Allow me the courtesy to share the following: I have been hanging around Planet Earth for roughly 45 years now, and have discovered an absolute truth of human existence, which is this: Anyone is equipped with the ability to believe anything they want to believe – at any given moment – whether it is productive or destructive – perceived as right or wrong – and whether or not the belief is rooted in fact or fiction.

When it comes to the 'human decision' to choose what we want to believe, the Power of Belief does not discriminate. It doesn't matter what ethnicity you are, what sex, religion, color of your skin, sexual orientation, what country you live in, or how you identify yourself – your capacity to believe whatever you want is completely up to you. For example, ask 100 people to offer their definition of god and you will most likely end up with about 100 different variations – even if they are from the same church. And, if you ask the same one hundred to describe their interpretation of 'love,' then you will be quite surprised when you end up with a wide range of answers; some selfish, some delusional, some altruistic and others unselfish – many, many, differing concepts in what people believe.

When I finally experienced the 'A-Ha moment' in relation to the Power of Belief for myself, I had a realization of paramount importance: I realized that how I came to believe, whatever it was I was choosing to believe, would be best suited for myself and everyone, if it had a logical foundation and based upon some reliable data, that I discovered in my own experience; not what someone told me to believe.

If I choose NOT to base my decisions on some logical process, then I would simply continue believing in things that may or may not be true – until, for instance, another authority figure, such as: parents, government, teachers, or religious leaders told me to believe something else. Or, better yet, until I started thinking for myself beyond conditioning I was subjected to from birth.

I vaguely recall a bittersweet memory from childhood: I was about 5 or 6 when I was finally told Santa Clause wasn't real, and neither was the Easter Bunny. Thank goodness! Could you imagine a 30 or 40 year old, walking into the gym to pump iron with the guys, then striking up a conversation about the chubby old white-bearded man who's going to personally deliver a new set of exercise equipment to your living room floor – in December – down the chimney you don't have? How embarrassing would that be? With respect to religious beliefs, many people have conversations just like that one, yet instead of Santa – it's Jesus or god – and instead of exercise equipment, the gift is a well-paying job.

I also have partial recollection from childhood of almost getting into a fist fight with a few friends when they told me Santa wasn't real, because: How could the most trusted people in my life, my parents, lie to me about that? What else have they lied about? Religion? God?

As I grew older, I noticed this trend: Parents and authority figures, such as government officials, teachers, religions, and politicians, telling me things that seemed to be misleading, or downright lies. Of course, I don't think the majority of 'misleadings' are obvious ones (like Santa), but more along the lines of passing down traditional mind habits and myths – that aren't true. I noticed that virtually all human beings were programmed by their parents and culture – those who governed and conditioned them with unreliable data, fictional stories, and behavioral patterns.

Could this 'passing down of beliefs systems' be the same conceptual process and psychological trend that allows religious ideologies and wars, self destructive corporate practices, and maladapted governmental traditions to persist in a culture – for what seems to be, forever! And, is this the same way how the fictional belief system of 'who I think I am' was birthed?

My last few statements mildly alludes to a fundamental

A LOVING INVITATION TO LOOK WITHIN

reality of how religions and governments start and persist for centuries to millennia – leading to war, most of the time. It goes something like this: One group of people who believe one idea – that was passed down to them by their parents, which of course in their eyes is the right belief, finds themselves in opposition to another group, who believes a conflicting idea; which was handed down to them, by their parents – whom they believe to be the right idea. (This is quite confusing to keep track of.) All of this passing down of beliefs ends up in a conflict utilizing this unsolvable equation: "I'm right – you're wrong" VERSUS another "I'm right – you're wrong" mentality. The point is this: No body can win! Deeply embedded cultural habits which are passed down from generation to generation are very difficult to break; especially when we have been programmed what to believe by those raising us – whom we instinctively trust. As children, we had NO CHOICE what to believe. Of course, we believed our parents. And most of us STILL DO.

It appears that in order for us to change our deeply conditioned and embedded belief systems, in order to begin thinking for ourselves, we must first admit we have been unintentionally lied to, which in part, means: We must accept we were victims (to some degree) of betrayal – from our caregivers and authority figures and CULTURE. The fundamental formula which precedes changing the way we think is as follows: admission of the unintentional betrayal followed by radical forgiveness. The last statement sounds very familiar to the Christian Biblical quote Jesus theoretically spoke: "Forgive them, for they know not what they do." On a personal note, I like this quote; however, I do not believe that Jesus spoke it. I do, in fact, believe someone enlightened spoke it, but no one knows for sure…at least that's what I believe. (Are you getting the picture, yet?) Everything is about a belief that YOU get to CHOOSE.

So…where does this leave us now? One of my personal desires and impetus in writing this article was this: I really would like the reader to experience the "A-Ha moment" of realization about the Power of Belief, which states that anyone can believe whatever they want – regardless of anything – no hard evidence – no nothing.

Furthermore, our belief potential indicates that the human species has evolved the capability to rationalize anything – for any reason – no matter what. Sounds insane, doesn't it? Well…perhaps this is the only 'real truth' there is in the human experience that we all have in common. Redundantly speaking: You have the innate capacity and ability to believe absolutely anything you want – regardless of any one else's belief, AND you get to choose to believe facts VERSUS fiction – and anything else in between.

Lastly, if we choose to believe the information above, then we may be caught in a catch 22 about our entire paradigm of consciousness; (Or may I say a catch 22 of imagination?) Nonetheless, when we observe with keen eyes, awareness, and unencumbered freethinking, our conclusion may be this: The Power of Belief has become a major hindrance in our evolutionary stage of developing into a human species – a species who is trying to become reasonable, logical, compassionate, altruistic, peaceful, and loving.

Perhaps, as individuals, developing our own 'checks and balance' system for choosing what to believe would help unmask the inherent risks of belief; you know: a conscious methodology which is self imposed by our own self – by our own being – beyond brain – beyond mind – within our own experience – beyond belief.

Watch the Thinker

Preface: Please hold the following in consciousness while reading this article: Your mind will most likely be trying to figure out and conceptualize what is written. These words only point to truth and are NOT truth. There is nothing written here that can be figured out; but, only realized and understood in the indescribable dimension of truth which exists beyond mind and form. Please also be aware that some combination of meditation, yoga, and self inquiry methods most likely are essential to assisting your being in becoming open to a depth of stillness necessary to realize truth, that words of guidance offer.

By believing that suffering or having a midlife crisis is possible, ego is tricking you into thinking you currently have a self to begin with – a false identity that is in jeopardy (which is not you) – something that is capable of having a crisis; please hear this: it is only the belief in suffering which makes suffering possible; deeper yet, only a belief in a finite mind-made self causes suffering. In other words, if you think and believe in a mid-life crisis then you will most likely find yourself in one.

What experiences suffering is never your true nature. What you really are is incapable of suffering; incapable of fear; incapable of hatred; incapable of crises. What you 'really are' is incapable of believing – anything. Although not capable of believing, what appears to happen is that your truest nature is capable of adopting or identifying with a mind-made belief. Immediately following birth, our intuitive life essence, (that which we truly are), had no choice but to adopt or identify with believing thoughts, ideas, and concepts, as a means of surviving and navigating physical existence.

Please be open to this possibility: behind the scenes of any perceived crises, or suffering, is the witness to it – a physical-less, a form-less presence - your truest essence; the one who simply observes the crisis or suffering. Being the witness is like someone watching a movie who does not become emotionally involved with the characters; they simply pay attention and watch what is happening without reacting or associating. However, once you identify with the emotions of a character or the plot in a film, then you begin to suffer…notice this.

You see, the one that suffers is not your true essence. What suffers is the idea of the self which is rooted in survival self preservation (the mind). Suffering is actually a self preservation survival trait available only to help your physical form survive and persist in the world (mostly through avoidance?); please hear this: you are not the physical form, and thoughts are physical too – which you are not. In fact, you are not your mind, body, or emotion or memory. Let us honor suffering, however, because the suffering we endure is actually a beautiful part of your complex since it is designed to always protect your physical components; always trying to protect you using mind and thinking. However, there does come a point where suffering needs to be stopped if we are to live peacefully within.

Please see that 'trying' in the 'trying to protect' thinking mode is the obsession and compulsion to think, figure out, and analyze – which catalyzes suffering. Thinking, figuring out, and analyzing do not directly cause suffering, but the out-of-control compulsion to do so. It is very much like one thought arises, (which has the potential to be watched and simply let go without suffering), but the mind immediately begins obsessing about it in order to figure out how to integrate the thought into the system as a means of protection – based upon mis-information accumulated through years of conditioning; which amounts to a confused state of existence (more suffering).

Early on in your existence, ego adopted the names 'me,' 'my,' 'mine,' 'I,', 'myself,' and 'you.' And, what happened is your truest intuitive nature adopted and identified with the idea of those names as a physical form; meaning, you have bought into the story of a finite self named 'me.' If you did not adopt the belief that there is a self named, 'me,' in the first place, then it would be impossible to suffer or experience a crisis. Try this: examine the possibility there are two types of 'me;' one that is mind made and one rooted in an indescribable truth of existence – your boundless nature housed in stillness. Note that your true nature is changeless and incapable of believing, because believing is at the level of mind – which you are not. (You are here to use the mind NOT let the mind use you.) Existing beyond believing is more like deep knowing or understanding. Only that which your truest essence has identified with is what does the believing; what is doing the believing is the mind – not you.

In other words, there is a 'thinking self' (which you have adopted as 'myself') that we could call the believer; one who believes things merely out of conditioning. Before there was conditioning, there was 'you' who was never a self but a pure boundless piece of life – awareness beyond mind and thinking. Then, conditioning happened and the accumulation of information and data became your story of a fictional life titled, "I Am the Body and Mind."

Please note also, an ego trick is this: the ego believes there is a false self – the opposite of the true self - two side of the same mythological coin. Therefore, once you have become identified with the mind (which everyone has) until you dis-identify, then you will continually maintain the belief in both the false self and true self; both of which do not exist in reality – only in idea. The semantics here is difficult because even an enlightened being refers to itself as 'I' or 'me' at times. However, they are only using language as a tool of communicating information but not allowing that communication, words, and language to instill and reinforce an identity which does not exist. Bear in mind that every time you use those words like 'I' or 'me' then you are most likely reinforcing the problem. The ego or mind is the thinker; the one doing the believing or disbelieving in the distorted dimension of mind. So if you are not your mind, yet you are trying to use thinking, (which is mind), to figure out who the false self and true self is, then how will you ever see that you are NOT the thinker or the mind? You are neither the true self nor false self. (Pause here and contemplate the last few sentences.)

Moreover, please know this: you are not the one who believes. In other words, if you believe there is a false self then you believe there is a true self, thus guaranteeing duality; meaning, you are identified with the 'believer' which does not exist except as a manufactured component of mind. Point to the believer (right now) and describe the believer without words or concepts. Can you see the believer?

Perhaps, this will help clarify. The process was and is this: Data is input into the mind, then mind processes it and a belief option is created, then your true essence immediately adopts the belief as 'true,' typically. For example, do you think you are ugly or pretty? Answer: none of the above or anything else in between. All answers to this question are false beliefs (even the answer I gave.) This adoption of beliefs has been accumulating since birth and has become an unconscious identity or identities.

One of the clearest ways to describe the aforementioned is that you are currently not aware you have options to either adopt and identify with beliefs; or NOT adopt and identify with them. The challenge is this: believing is all you know at the moment. We must create space in your essence (using meditation, meditative self inquiry, or yoga methods) in order to see this process of believing is happening so quickly that you don't see the option not to engage with thoughts. We have great difficulty seeing there is a choice, and allow thoughts and beliefs to merely pass right through consciousness. There appears to be resistance to allowing stuck thoughts to go, and not giving energy to new thoughts as you watch them arise…then observe them pass away into nothingness, whence they came.

Again, capable at the level of mind, is believing and disbelieving, yet there is space in between the two; we will call this space of stillness, possibility; the possibility to not entertain thoughts or any component of mind. Be open to the possibility you can exist beyond belief, without believing or disbelieving anything, in a dimension of possibility where experiencing truth beyond mind is always available here now.

In closing, as mentioned at the beginning in the preface, what is most likely occurring in your mind right now is that you are confused – due to 'trying to figure out' what this article is about. This is a great opportunity to witness the 'thinker' which is the process of 'trying to figure out;' the voice which is operating at the level of mind; this thinker is NOT you. What your true nature is – is that of a witness – the one who watches, notices, and observes those voices which are trying to figure everything out.

Random Prose

If it's not joy then it's not me. Joy is all there is – always – for no reason at all; but, if you need a reason...because joy is the possibility to realize joy is everything, and as long as you are still breathing then that possibility is available. Please know that even the possibility is NOT a belief; it is truth. One must look and see truth beyond believing – beyond perceiving – to witness the possibility.

Can you hear the voice of doubt – something that believes this possibility is not possible, which is disbelief, yet still a belief; the doubter who believes in suffering more than joy? Only that which is NOT you can believe or disbelieve truth. (As the watcher – You) Watch the doubter of truth (ego-mind), and watch disbelief and belief dissolve while truth arises – the essence of life – joy – You.

$$\alpha\ \alpha\ \alpha$$

Most people when they "think" they are taking a big leap into the abyss, allow themselves to be caught by something physical, like a job, a new husband or wife, change of address, any personal relationship, or money, etc.; because any major lifestyle change typically feels like a step into an abyss of letting go of some degree of control. Yet, with taking a big leap with regard to spiritual awakening, there is nothing physical to catch you – nothing – no thing – nothing to rely on or depend on for comfort and security.

There cannot be anything physical to catch you because the physical only begets more physical and the problem is the identification with all the components of body and mind (emotions, feelings, sensations, thoughts, and memories – which by their very nature are actually physical.) Therefore, if one continues to allow himself or herself to be caught by something physical then their ultimate nature will go unnoticed; your formless non physical essence will never be realized.

When a person takes an honest spiritual leap into the abyss, there can't be a net to catch you, because there is nothing (no physical self) that needs caught; and, what is 'wanting' to awaken is NOT physical. (What you really are is incapable of wanting – incapable of trying.) What you really are, without it being a question can be described this way: you really are formless and physical-less consciousness – which does not need caught – only seen and liberated.

α α α

Everyone appears to be waging war internally in one way or another, due to some form of belief. Then, many of us, if not all of us, are up in arms with the "I can't believe this is happening!" thought. The truth is that there really is absolutely nothing to get upset about - no matter what - because everyone is suffering from the ultimate belief which gives birth to all beliefs you are in opposition to. And, that belief is that you are a self – that you matter – that you are someone important – that you are NOT insignificant. You may matter, but never in the way in which you THINK you matter.

α α α

It is impossible for anything to be other than it is. Whether it is a thought, emotion, feeling, memory, sensation, perception, idea, judgment, hate, love, greed, etc...anything. Resistance to what is - is my piece of consciousness handing over the reigns to ego-mind to hold on - instead of allowing everything to be as it is - beyond interpretation - beyond judgment. Consciousness is not a concept and indescribable. (Note: Right Now, see if you can watch your mind assigning a meaning to the word consciousness.) Are you willing, ready, and able to realize truth beyond the comprehending mind, here now?

α α α

Sadness, My Teacher, Thank You.

Sadness falls upon me as reality of loosing the misperception of yet another friend is imminent. Or, am I merely shedding another layer of delusion revealing truth within? Yes...A revelation which births clarity that there is no such thing as loss, but only liberation which illuminates the illusion of darkness within.

Thank you perception of loss which has taught me to feel as humans do, and empathize with those lost in the physical realm where I have laid dormant for many decades.

I am allowed to be free now. I have always been allowed to be free but have not been aware. I am allowed to let go. I am allowed to notice, appreciate, embrace, honor, love, then let go of all mind constructs, memories, thoughts, emotions, and projections.

I am allowed to relinquish all falsehoods marring me in the quicksand of suffering so I can swim in the omnipotent sea of truth. Thank you humility for teaching me surrender. Thank you Loss...for pointing the way. Thank you, sadness, for showing me that I am nothing.

Our Collective Human Family
One Earth—One Community

As we awaken to existence beyond our instinctual selfish nature and survivalist mentality, on both an individual and collective level, we see the world evolving in multiple dimensions, simultaneously. Intelligence is evolving. Emotions are evolving. Information Technologies are evolving. The way we interact is evolving! Your mind is evolving, too! Which means: Everyone's mind is evolving; thus, creating a global transformation in thought, communication, and behavior—which we now understand as a paradigm shift in consciousness - OR - 'Collective Evolution.'

This shift within our mind, body, and soul (however you personally define them) is creating a unified collective awakening, across the globe! Deep within the minds and hearts of more individuals than ever before, (especially our youth), is deep yearning for higher purpose and need to feel connected with something greater than our own egoic selfish desires. Many of us have consciously evolved to a point where we are looking beyond outdated ideas of god, government, and social conformities, and seeking to establish a permanent relationship with our Higher Consciousness, within—who strives to bond with the entire human race as a whole.

Our global shift in awareness is inspiring many human beings to examine their existence, and question the unconscious habitual mind programs that have been conditioned into us. Many of us are tired of making sense of contradictory ideas pervading our society which are leading us astray on a personal, national, and global level. We are looking for logical means of understanding why the human race thinks and behaves the way we do; in other words, many of us are trying to get a handle on our current level of awareness and looking for solutions beyond indoctrinated cultural norms and dogma—so we can awaken within to collectively improve our world and nurture our home—Planet Earth. This is great NEWS! And PROGRESS! In order to make the world a better place, many of us are passionately seeking new perspectives and internal answers to our mutual human endeavors—are you?

Furthermore, there is a vast array of self defeating beliefs emanating in the world extending from religion, consumerism, and government—which have been adopted as truths within both our individual and collective mind—and we have accepted them as 'the norm.' For example, the idea money and god can solve all of our problems—both foreign and domestic. Reality is proving, rather, consciousness is demanding the human species realize that many outdated concepts once invented to solve our problems are no longer working for us. The destructive trends and damaging consequences of our human species, to ourselves and the planet, is proving we need to change our thinking to more sustainable core values. Moreover, we are beginning to realize that many of our social structures, habitualized cultural thought processes, and normalized unconscious actions are built upon a foundation of maladapted principles; such as: depletion, obsolescence, greed, and power, to name a few. This mindset must change.

The good news is: We are awakening! Within each and every one of us is our individual heart and mind evolving into something I describe as our Higher Self—which is our most authentic and finest being that is allowing our best human quality to express itself—Altruism. In Plain English, Altruism could be described as a new level of consciousness that constantly brings forth the following Interdependent thought: "What is spiritually beneficial for me is spiritually beneficial for everyone and our planet?" versus the "What's in it for me?" attitude of the ego.

Perhaps, we have reached a stage in our evolutionary melting pot of Biology, Physics, Chemistry, Psychology, and Spirituality, where a new gene, the Altruistic Gene, is becoming dominant in the collective gene pool of the human species. And, whatever this wonderful shift in human greatness is—we know something is harnessing the innate human desire to be: kind, generous, compassionate, and unselfish—more often—with others—and most importantly— within our own self.

This amazing moment in time along the continuum of evolution is proving that we are, indeed, beginning to understand that the human race is interconnected in some way. Thanks to the Information Superhighway, (the Internet), the entire globe has access to virtually everything and everybody! WOW! We are definitely learning how interconnected we really are. What a spectacular time to be alive!

As compassionate human beings who are growing into awareness, before losing ourselves by trying to 'save the world,' our innate Altruistic tendencies are inspiring us to focus on our inner being first, regardless of where we live or the culture we subscribe to. By focusing inward, what naturally develops is the awareness (and consciousness) to see that many of our collective habits and cultural practices are destroying our planet, and damaging our food supply. And, how each of us may be contributing to the same problems we complain about, and that we must do something about them.

New and innovative philosophies, like Clean and Green Energy, and Planet Conservation are headed to the forefront of our global priorities. New Age educational programs and industries, such as Permaculture, are setting new examples for us to follow; which educates and encourages us to develop sustainable food sources and healthy living. Many flourishing Intentional Communities are guided by these principles, thus leading by example 'a new way of living the change.' These common sense Humanistic tactics and strategies are being adopted by our youth, too, who are literally our future. Of course, since our children of today will be the leaders of tomorrow's corporations and governments, by teaching them new and improved cultural habits now, we will see Interdependent and Altruistic values reflected in their future decisions; which will affect everyone. Properly educating and conditioning our youth with Humanistic Principles is paramount to the happiness and survival of the Human Race, and uniting and healing our world.

In closing, allow me to share that millions of people on Earth are awakening to greater purpose by cultivating their most compassionate and loving higher consciousness—their Higher Self. As easily witnessed via Social Media Resources, whether it be watching clips displaying random acts of kindness or videos showing enlightened beings pointing at truth, reading New Age ideas from Facebook pages, or posting inspiring messages on a blog, we see a coming together of Altruism like never before, in history. There has never been a time (other than now) where we could witness incredible Digital Technologies and astounding Psychological and Spiritual growth potential coming together in such a concerted effort—inspiring us to improve our mutual human condition. We are being propelled into a new world—an Interdependent World with a new understanding that we all need one another. We are finally beginning to realize that there is only: One Home—Planet Earth and One Community — Our Collective Human Family.

Misunderstanding Presence

Do you want to be at peace, now? Or, would you rather worry about the future? Do you want to be at peace, in the present, now? Or, feel ashamed about the past? If your answer is: "Be at peace, now, in the present," then why are you choosing suffering?

Our fear, worry, shame, hence, all of our suffering are beautiful survival tactics housed in what we call ego - our survival system – a mind system which helps us navigate all practical aspects of life. Housed in ego-mind are emotional tactics, thought strategies, and mental habits, beginning the moment we left the womb, in response to the external environment; which become vital survival cognitive and behavioral adaptations; none of these mental components have anything to do with the here-now, the timeless present moment - what we really are before conditioning.

All survival system components are (what I deem) non-presence; meaning: they do not exist in reality - not in the here-now, yet only in mental formations of past and mental projections of future. Therefore, fictional memories of past and imaginary projections of future create mind static and cognitive white noise; none of which are in relation to here-now. All mind chatter is non-presence and does not exist in reality, except in mind, thus causing suffering; mind is NOT you. However, if you choose to identify as your thoughts and mind voices as your mind-made idea of you, then you are buying into a fictional story of who you are; because, nothing exists beyond here-now – not even you..

Wrapped up in the egoic myth of past and future is the illusion of control. In a way, (and pushing aside that speaking of these things typically reinforces the false belief in time), past, future, and present are all the same thing – yet non existent.

Can you point to the past with your finger? Show me. If you point to a picture on the wall, you are mistaken, that picture is in the here-now. Can you point to the future? Show me. If you point to the calendar of events for next week, then you are mistaken - the calendar is now.

Can you point to the now? Yes! Show me!

It is all around you, within and without…here! NOW!

Quotes II

If I have to ask, then it's not me – watch the one asking – this wakeful awareness watching, (who I really am) is incapable of speaking or thinking.

α

The illusion of control is sustained through believing in an illusory self – hence belief systems are formed which consciousness somehow adopts as 'itself' until consciousness sees the illusion thus recognizing itself.

α

Now is the miracle that everyone must see.

α

You matter, but not in the way in which you think you matter.

α

The moment I honestly admitted to myself how unconscious I was – was the exact same moment I began to awaken.

α

It seems to be that one must learn to feel as a matter of reclaiming autonomy over body and mind, before one can simply be.

α

Be grateful and appreciative for what is, instead of ungrateful and resentful for what isn't.

α

Mind is unbiased to any notion of right and wrong; it only wants to maintain itself by creating false identities which believe they are in control, and whether or not those identities are perceived as good or bad.

α

Aren't you tired of entertaining and defending your illusion of suffering?

α

If it's physical then you can guarantee it's a distraction from truth.

α

Comparison is judgment's twin;
and both sustain suffering.

α

Be compassion, love, and humility – lose interest in suffering.

α

If a person never admits how unconscious they are, then what are their chances for ever becoming conscious?

α

Procrastination is an illusory form of control - keeping one stuck in illusory time.

α

Don't overlook here now.

α

It takes no energy to let go, only to hold on;
and, what we hold onto most...is suffering.

α

One must drop all mind-made conditional stories, beliefs, notions, concepts, and ideas of god, before one can know God.

α

Meditation and Yoga are always, now.

α

The mind has the capability to justify anything,
which includes justifying destructive
tendencies or productive ones.

α

Realizing Untruth

What does 'being' mean? We use words to point at truth and in this instance the truth of 'being.' However, there are no words to describe the indescribable, i.e. 'being,' and trying to answer the question in the first sentence of this paragraph (with content) ironically negates your quest for inner peace. Let us offer a method of sorts to undo some conditioning which may be blocking truth from your conscious awareness, by supposing we realize untruth. And, untruth is what isn't. And, what may help direct one inward and provide clarity is the following:

Not engaging the associative or analytical or identification process of the mind; not obsessing; not engaging in emotions; realizing that your true nature is something completely different from the mostly unconscious identification processes you have been engaged in your entire life; realizing current roles and identities you have been practicing are mostly unconscious illusions and a deterrent from seeing truth within; realizing that emotions feel real BUT are not truth – even happiness is not what you think it is, because all feelings, emotions, sensations, thoughts, ideas, memories...everything arises, stays for a while, then passes away - thus all is bound by the illusion of time. Become open to the possibility - then realizing that time is a mind construct which can be dropped. With time, there is excitement; without time there is peace.

Realizing that inner peace and excitement are separate things, and realizing there is a difference between conditional happiness (cause of suffering) versus unconditional happiness (pure joy); realizing the difference between circumstance and state of mind; realizing you have a type of control (but not really) over your mind; realizing the true present moment and what it is not; realizing how you perceive things is a choice; realizing the external does not determine your state of mind; realizing you always have within everything you need to be at peace.

And, in order to allow the fear of emptiness to dissolve and realize selflessness, you must let go of what you do not need – what you do not need are hindrances to truth – let go of untruths.

Parents – Forgive Yourselves
You are bearing the same wounds as your Children.

Preface: Allow me to share something which may sound completely untrue or deeply confusing, but here it goes: In truth, there is really no such thing as forgiveness in the sense in which we think there is; this is because (in truth) there is no such thing as mistakes, hence, nothing for anyone to be forgiven for – not even yourself. However, at the level of mind: forgiving, making amends, and admitting perceived mistakes, can and often does, allow stuck energy in the form of self judgment to move and dissolve – opening the door to higher conscious understanding, beyond judgment. Most people have internalized that they, themselves, (false selves invented by ego which they have identified with), are a mistake. Please note: as we work through what appears to be natural stages of human development via forgiveness, something that must be discerned is the difference between making mistakes via behavior versus feeling internally like you are a mistake. In truth, there is nothing wrong with anyone, AND of course, it is impossible for anyone to be a mistake, ever, no matter what.

A LOVING INVITATION TO LOOK WITHIN

Imagine bringing a child into this world; a world that seems so relentlessly cruel. Everywhere you turn there appears to be another form of subtle to gross neglect; because no one seems to know any better, not even you. You want your child to be loved, but you find your own past wounds have you trapped in survival mode – limiting your compassion and understanding. Your concept of what 'life is supposed to be' has you in its powerful grip, and will not let go.

You feel in your heart that you could be doing better raising your child, but doing your best does not seem good enough, even though you think you should. Fear of not raising your child properly seems to cycle despair greater and greater, and guilt and shame generated from loathsome feelings of not being good enough, in the eyes of your child, strengthens.

This relentless cycle of internal pain continues and becomes a learned behavior passed on to your child, because in their most formative years, you are all they have, and the way you speak and act, is all they know. In this way, as parents, we pass on our wounds, shame, fear, guilt, and false beliefs, to the next generation, unconsciously.

At times, thoughts pass through your mind, some completely true, some partially – of knowing your child (has been or is) neglected in some way. Perhaps it is lack of attention, lack of compassion, lack of appreciation, lack of understanding, lack of empathy, lack of validation, lack of presence, lack of listening, lack of 'just letting them be as they are,' lack of cultivating their best qualities, or lack of supporting who they want to become, lack of something – which is depriving them of growing up as fearless and shameless adults capable of emanating selfless compassion unto the world; to some degree they become wounded, because that's simply what happens as a natural stage of human development.

Then imagine seeing your child growing up into an adult, but that adult is not there. Due to harsh realities of childrearing, each parent is subjected to personal limitations, yielding offspring who lack full emotional autonomy and individuality; (and collectively speaking), yielding unconscious societies restricted from cultivating the most conscious human beings possible.

Both individually, and as a species, we appear to have arrived, inevitably, where familial and societal belief systems are projecting the illusion of independence, thus breeding more fear perpetuating the survive at all costs mentality; especially, when children are pushed from the nest and ill equipped to confront what life is really like.

Perhaps, the child already saw the bigger picture of life, once, but this knowing was conditioned out of them at a very early age, much like what happened to you. It is not your fault nor your child's – nor your parents'. Most of us unconsciously think (lacking awareness), parents included, that life is all about suffering; when it does not need to be. Suffering does help us awaken, however, we need to liberate ourseslves from the cyclical belief system of suffering, which states: In order to be happy I must suffer first, and vice versus.

With a compassionate heart, take a moment and think of the internal pain you may feel when you realize the biggest reason your child suffers is because of your perception of poor parenting; rather, some degree of inadequate parenting. Fueled by your own internal pain, self accusations, self criticisms, self blame, and self judgment, most likely held you back, tethering you to survival mode, which was then passed on to your children, to some extent; a practice unconsciously bequeathed to you by your parents and upbringing.

Imagine the clarity these insights offer, and self acceptance you must embrace, in order to look the reality of parenting directly in the eyes…to see that all wounds, both yours and your children's, are no ones fault; yet, an amends may be necessary. Now, imagine the courage it may require to apologize to your child, yet more importantly, the heartfelt courage to forgive yourself, first.

Imagine the humility, which is readily available, to nurture your own wounds, in order to cultivate inner love and exude compassion to all. To let go of judgment when you look into your child's eyes, because they are not doing what you want them to do...to let go of judgment when you look into your own eyes. Why not allow your children to be just as they are, because forcing them may cause unnecessary pain, self judgment – basically a form of detrimental learned oppression.

Most of us are blind to the suffering we inflict upon our sons and daughters, because when you see their suffering, then you see your own suffering; and, we are afraid to address our own internal strife and unattended sorrow, inflicted by our own parents. When you see your children's pain, then you see your mistakes; and, when you witness the fires of their life then, you see you were inevitably the match. It is ok. It is not your fault. It is no one's fault... and...there is no fire or match – only possibilities to learn and grow – to let go of self judgment.

Now, think of the reality of what we deem adulthood... the truth to what it means to be 'all grown up.' In reality, regardless of your parental inadequacies and emotional deficiencies that molded your child, when your child reaches a certain age, they must then find their own way. No matter what you have done or how badly you judge yourself as a parent, let it go. Your child, too, like yourself, must take responsibility for their own life, at some point.

Your children, too, must learn self compassion, and how to forgive themselves, ultimately allowing them to forgive you. If necessary, imagine embracing this wisdom and holding your child in your arms with loving kindness the next time they enter your presence. Imagine running to them and cloaking them with open acceptance and well tempered humility. Imagine caressing and greeting them with non judgment.

Imagine…the next time he or she shows up at your door, you offer a refuge of security, compassion, and understanding in such a way…a way you rarely experienced in your own life, but are now equipped to share. And, before they depart again on their own unique journey of life, imagine empowering them with the strength to conquer the world at every turn; because, you finally offered them what was missing, your own self forgiveness which freed you to offer full acceptance, humility, compassion, and loving kindness, to them.

Imagine this…if only for a moment…

…then imagine that you are the parent – the parent of a child who is damaged, broken, hopeless, and helpless. The parent of a child who has cloaked themselves with hardened layers of fear, anger, frustration, guilt, and shame – a child whose primary instinct is to protect him or herself at all costs…to run and hide.

Imagine this…if only for a moment…

…then imagine…imagine that child is you – your wounded child within, whose voice has been suppressed for many years, and is screaming for some attention – to be noticed

– to be validated – to be seen – that you do matter and exist.

Then imagine this...there is NO child. There is no child because that child is you...a person who is responsible to love itself no matter what happened. You are the lover of you. You are the caretaker of your very own wounds. You are love itself – a loving presence beyond words, descriptions, and conditions. Acknowledging that you were never allowed to grow up fully into the compassionate loving being you already are, will open the door to stop projecting your hurt onto your children and others, no matter how subtle.

Be aware of your wounds, and when emotions, feelings, and sensations of suffering knock on your door, let them in and embrace them. Douse them in love, cloak them in forgiveness, empower them with self compassion, and then let them go on their way. Let them go – it is no longer your responsibility to protect your suffering. Allow them to diffuse out into the world.

And, when your own child comes home, then nurture them in the ways you were never taught – but now understand. Love them in the way you never knew, then let them go. That child needs to move on and grow up on their own – give them space he or she needs.

Give yourself permission to let them go. Give yourself permission to let yourself go and live your life carefree of your own wounds. Let your identity of suffering you have adopted, die. Let the identities of both 'bad parent' and 'good parent' go – so you can be born anew.

Now...don't imagine...don't imagine anything...make letting go a reality...make non judgment a reality...allow your understanding and compassionate nature radiate.

It is time to forgive yourself, allow yourself to breathe, and love. Parents...forgive yourselves.

The Myth of Self and Suffering

So, who wants to be in control? You, your self, your ego? Please see that ego-mind is nothing but a survival mechanism of mental projections which has nothing to do with what you really are. You are not a mind-made self because the notion of self creates separation, and nothing is separate from life – none of the mind-made selves we create. Please know this: What you really are (true self) is incapable of feeling isolated, separate, and alone. So, which 'you' wants to be in control…mind-made you OR truth you? Who wants to be in control…some illusory self? Do you want to control things on the inside, on the outside, or both?

Tell me…when was the last time you controlled any thing, person, your feelings, or whatever? Please share. Describe to me your control – all aspects of its nature. And, tell me about this self, too! Mind-made self yearns to know things and describe itself, especially its accomplishments; whereas, true self knows itself cannot be described, and is not interested in doing so.

Let me tell you a story. There was once a woman named Preeti who grew up in a family whose tradition was worshiping unicorns. For centuries, her family had created and passed down statues of horse-like creatures, each with a single horn on their head. All village families would perform daily unicorn worshiping rituals in the privacy of their homes. On one special day of each year, the entire village would gather, and for 3 consecutive days would celebrate unicorn powers bestowed to their people and universe.

As Preeti matured in age, she became very concerned about the shenanigans regarding worshiping unicorns. She could never see the power they gave the people. The people in the next village over, who worshipped cows, seemed to have the same problems her village had. When her village flooded so did all the nearby villages. When there was a drought then all crops failed in the surrounding fields, too. When Preeti was only 8 years old she decided to search for the power of the unicorn - to prove to herself if unicorns exist - to really experience their power first hand - hence, not merely believing what people taught her to beleive.

On this particular day she set out to find unicorn power. Because most children are very wise, she deduced it would be a good idea to find a unicorn and ask where it gets its power. She ventured out searching for unicorns and did not return for a week. When she returned, she asked her parents and several people in the village if anyone had ever seen a unicorn, and of course, no one had. From then on she began questioning the entire notion of unicorns - that perhaps unicorns were merely a myth - an illusion.

As she grew older, her childlike mind became more deeply distorted, conditioned, and masked over with many untruths. At the age of fourteen she set off again to find a unicorn; because now, she was old enough to explore great distances. She decided to make it her mission in life - to find a unicorn in order to discover its power.

After 4 decades of searching, at the age of 54, after traveling the entire world, she returned to the village where she was raised. Her journey, although imparting enormous global adventure, left her miserable at every turn because she couldn't find a unicorn anywhere. After years of searching, the people in her village were still conducting the same unicorn rituals - nothing had changed there. With a dispassionate heart, she decided to sit for a day in receptive silence and meditative self inquiry. After many hours, her eyes popped open, she looked at the sky and began laughing hysterically, repeating, "There is no such thing as unicorns!" "There is no such thing as unicorns!"

Similarly, to the unicorn story above is the story of the illusory mind-made self, and the story of control, and the story of suffering and misery. They are all illusions - all details of the same myth - the myth that there is an 'I' (false self) to begin with. The mind-made notion of 'I' and suffering, which have masked our true nature, are merely projections of the mind (the ego), and the greatest contributor to fear, worry, and misery. In our unconscious they lurk, we think, BUT, there is nothing lurking only more thinking which sustains the thinking, which is why the suffering persists. We will never find the one who is suffering (the I) because mind-made 'I' isn't really there - there are no unicorns. In the story, Preeti thought there were unicorns and spent her life trying to prove it, when they don't even exist. Each of us do this same thing, trying to prove that our mind-made self (which is a myth) exists, and that it has value, worth, and needs validated. The only thing there is – is a fictional story of suffering – a fictional story of control – a myth of unicorns – a myth of 'I'; and, what brings great misery and sorrow is our impossible quest to find those myths.

The suffering is a phantom, a myth, a fictional story, all playing the role of a unicorn – a false self – which does not exist. If we continue searching for a cure to the suffering, searching for a self, yet there is no suffering and no self, then how will suffering ever go away? The same energy in the searching is the same energy which allows the suffering to live on – as an illusion – as a unicorn. Would you search the universe looking for a unicorn – anything which does not exist? The more searching for a solution to end suffering (myth) ONLY means more suffering. These illusions persists until we see the truth for ourselves through direct experience – within – that there is no self and no such thing as control. By choosing to entertain the myth of suffering by believing in unicorns, misery, and mind-made self, in the first place, the quest for the illusory source of suffering, somehow, empowers the suffering to perpetuate.

Are you willing to sit in receptive silence until you see the myth? Are you open to the possibility that suffering can indeed end, altogether? Any voice of resistance is NOT you. Any voice that says, "I don't get it!" is NOT you. Observe the voices. You are the observer – the awareness who observes everything, NOT the mind-made 'I' who is constantly in doubt.

A Guru's Parable

A man went to his spiritual guru and said, "I keep scratching my mosquito bite but it won't stop itching." The guru replied, "Hmm. Do you have any other questions?"

A month past and the man sought out to ask another question. He found the guru and asked, "I can't cut as much wood as I used to when I was young. I always chop wood for hours and then have a sore back for days. Can't I heal myself quicker?" The guru said, "Hmm. Do you have any other questions?"

A week went by and the man asked the guru another question. He spoke, "Master, I have been asking you questions for years now, and the only response you ever give me is 'hmm.' How can anything change in my life if you never tell me anything else?" To this statement, the guru responded by saying, "Hmm. Do you have any other questions?"

The man went away angry and did not return for many years. Then one day, he found enough courage to confront his guru. He asked, "Master please - I need guidance! Why haven't you told me anything other than hmm and ask if I have any other questions?'"

The guru looked at him directly in his eyes and contemplated for a moment, and gently spoke, "Dear friend - many years ago I offered you the 'one' answer to all questions you put before me, but I do not think you were listening."

"No. I don't remember," the man hurriedly replied.

"Are you ready to listen now, my friend?" the guru whispered.

"Yes. Yes. I want to speed up my spiritual awakening Master. My life is very discouraging all of the time and the years keep dragging on."

The guru leaned in with a heartfelt and compassionate stare and spoke lovingly, "Your spiritual journey is not a race with an end, but a process of opening your heart and letting go. There is nothing to speed up. If you are suffering, then the first step is to drop doing whatever you are doing that is causing your suffering; and, only you can realize for yourself what is at the root of your suffering – what you must let go."

The guru went on to say, "I spoke these exact words to you when you asked me your very first question decades ago. Are you finally ready (and willing) to embrace and realize this message? These words are all you need to know for now until you realize for yourself what is causing you to suffer. Do you understand?"

The man replied, "I think so Master - I think so. So I must be open to letting go?"

The guru said, "Hmm. Do you have any other questions?"

Uncertainty

Listening to the laughing wind sailing through
the forgotten forest of my life. Is it mocking me?
With every step amidst the forest floor are the rustling
leaves I hear poking fun at my hidden past?
Do they hold the secrets, which only strangers masquerading as decaying matter know the answers to?
Are they posing? Have they forgotten?
Do they know?
Are the dying branches snickering at my hopeless uncer-
tainties which seem to find no rest? And, haunt me?
Or, is the wind simply whispering a chuckle of breath,
unencumbered, without judgment, criticism, or blame…
… for ever-present air knows there is no such thing as
past or future, or multiple present moments, and nothing
to worry about in the here now, as presence.

Letting Go of the Story of We

There is no 'we' in the same way there is no 'I.' The challenge is that our programming, language, and communication has already installed a meaning of these words in our brains; and, our minds have adopted a fictional story of 'we,' which must be dissolved before the truth of 'we' is seen.

In truth, there is no 'I' only a universal 'we.' However, at the moment, most everyone is looking through the mind filtered story of 'we' and story of 'I' - both of which block truth of universal 'we.' Allow me to mention, too, that this fictional dichotomy of 'us' and 'them' and 'me' and 'them' creates duality; causing a delusional idea of separation from universal 'we' which everything fundamentally is. (Please be open to discerning the difference between mind-made-story-we and indescribable universal truth-we.)

A clever language trick of ego-mind is to convince us that 'we' (story-we) must do things together (as a family, state, religious belief, species, etc.) while feeling isolated and alone, hence needing to form a 'we' to combat these feelings. So, no matter what is thought in terms of unity, when one is looking at unity as 'we' (meaning all of us I(s) must join together) then there is a very subtle unconscious reinforcement of the problem. The problem is that in order for there to be a 'we' then there must be separate I(s) to form an individual 'we.' These ego tricks sustain the illusion of separation by inventing and adopting the story of separate I(s). Again, in truth, there is only the idea of 'I' and 'We' because they are mental constructs; AND, truth (meaning all life forms) happened before the mind began conjuring up things.

One may be thinking as 'I' who is bringing together more I(s) to form a 'we' – which sounds wonderful for unity – all the while not knowing that what is occurring is NOT unity (in truth); but, only a covert ego tactic of continuing separation, simply because the 'I' does not want to feel alone. Please see there are no I(s) in truth thus nothing to join together to form a 'we.' And, no 'I' (in truth) which can feel alone.

'I' and 'We' (causing suffering) can only exist in the illusory dimension of mind, but not in the true dimension of existence – a dimension of true union – the dimension of heart where 'all is all' beyond the concept of 'I' and 'we' – absolute union – before mind.

Moreover, to the mind there is always a 'we' because in order for there to be a 'we' there has to be a whole bunch of I(s); which inherently means there must be separation between the I(s). And, when there is separation there is no union, yet in truth, everything is fundamentally already union – one. In other words, you must be thinking you are separate for even the notion of 'I' or 'we' to be in your mind; (or, you would be enlightened and never suffer again.)

Now, since the majority of human beings are currently identified with mind and body, meaning that each one of us 'thinks' we are nothing more than mind and body (the birth of I), then how we speak and communicate is filtered through the mind, hence, filtered through the 'I' and 'we' thought forms; which were conditioned into mind. Therefore, when we continue speaking or thinking in those terms, for example with 'I statements' and 'we statements' then we are constantly reinforcing separation, not unity; and, we are not even aware of this mind game we have bought into long ago. Words are for communication purposes only, not to adopt, identify, conceptualize, or believe as truths.

For example, one may say, "We must join together to create a better world." The one who is saying this does NOT realize that the entire whole of existence is already 'one' in perfect harmony – not separate – so why would that statement even apply? The answer is that in the dimension of mind, (the mind) makes statements of joining together using 'I' and 'we' language to fool ourselves into thinking we are separate, somehow, from all of existence.

YET in truth, the only dimension there is, in reality, is

reality itself; where one does not try to join things together, and the belief (illusion) of separation does not – cannot exist. How clever for the fundamental problem (a belief in separation) to sustain itself than to convince you the world must unite...this idea guarantees the illusion of separation (which is the fundamental cause of suffering.)

Another way to look at this is to consider the possibility that it is feasible to 'understand something' without the use of thinking, concepts, or mind. In other words, listen with your heart which is there underneath all of the thinking; your stillness – your true essence – before learning happened – which is already one with all that is – in absolute union with all creation both animate and inanimate.

Is every droplet of water in the ocean a separate 'I'? Or, is the droplet simply an integral part of something bigger – the ocean? Is the droplet an 'I' and the ocean the 'we'? So, again, is the droplet simply an integral part (absolute union already) of something bigger (absolute union already) – where union is the entire whole of existence (already absolute union)?

If you are the droplet, then what are you missing?

If it's not Joy - It's not me.
Direct your attention inward while reading this allowed to yourself.

If it's not joy – it's not me.
If it's not humility – it's not me.
If it's not compassion – it's not me.
If it's not love – it's not me.
If it's not peace – it's not me.
If it's not grace – it's not me.

This One must let go of belief in joy – to realize this one's true nature – infinite joy.
This One must let go of belief in humility – to realize this one's true nature – infinite humility.
This One must let go of belief in compassion – to realize this one's true nature – infinite compassion.
This One must let go of belief in love – to realize this one's true nature – infinite love.
This One must let go of belief in peace – to realize this one's true nature – infinite peace.
This One must let go of belief in grace – to realize this

one's true nature – infinite grace.

If it's judgment – it's not me.
If it's comparing – it's not me.
If it's analyzing – it's not me.
If it's doubting – it's not me.
If it's hating – it's not me.

If it's a feeling or thought of separation – it's not me.
If it's a feeling or thought of loneliness – it's not me.
If it's a feeling or thought of isolation – it's not me.
If it's a feeling or thought of abandonment – it's not me.
If it's shame – it's not me.

This One must let go of belief in need to judge – to realize this one's true nature – absence of judgment.
This One must let go of belief in need for comparing – to realize this one's true nature – absence of comparing.
This One must let go of belief in need for analyzing – to realize this one's true nature – absence of analyzing.
This One must let go of belief in need to doubt – to realize this one's true nature – absence of doubt.
This One must let go of belief in need to hate – to realize this one's true nature – absence of hate.

This One must let go of belief in thought of separation

– to realize this one's true nature – absence of separation.
This One must let go of belief in thought of loneliness
– to realize this one's true nature – absence of loneliness.
This One must let go of belief in thought of isolation
– to realize this one's true nature – absence of isolation.
This One must let go of belief in thought of abandonment – to realize this one's true nature – absence of abandonment.
This One must let go of belief in shame – to realize this one's true nature – absence of shame.

If it's looking to past – it's not me.
If it's looking to future – it's not me.
If it's urgent – it's not me.
If it's anticipating – it's not me.
If it's afraid – it's not me.
If it's worry – it's not me

This One must let go of belief in need for past – to realize this one's true nature – indescribable here-now.
This One must let go of belief in need for future – to realize this one's true nature – indescribable presence.
This One must let go of belief in need for urgency – to realize this one's true nature – indescribable stillness.
This One must let go of belief in need for anticipating – to realize this one's true nature – indescribable peace.

This One must let go of belief in need
for fear – to realize this one's true
nature – indescribable unshakeable calm.

This One must let go of belief in need for
worry – to realize this one's true
nature – indescribable absence of worry.

If it's thinking – it's not me.
If it's doing – it's not me.
If it's suffering – it's not me.

This One must let go of belief in need for thinking – to
realize this one's true nature – watching the thinking.
This One must let go of belief in need for doing – to
realize this one's true nature – watching the doing.
This One must let go of belief in need for suffering – to
realize this one's true nature – incapable of suffering.

If it's physical – it's not me.
If it's a thought – it's not me.
If it's a feeling – it's not me.
If it's a memory – it's not me.
If it's a future projection – it's not me.
If it's a sensation – it's not me.
If it's an emotion – it's not me.

If it's mind – it's not me.

This One must let go of identification as (body) physical self – to realize this one's true nature.
This One must let go of identification as thoughts – to realize this one's true nature.
This One must let go of identification as feelings – to realize this one's true nature.
This One must let go of identification as memory – to realize this one's true nature.
This One must let go of identification as future projections – to realize this one's true nature.
This One must let go of identification as sensations – to realize this one's true nature.
This One must let go of identification as emotions – to realize this one's true nature.
This One must let go of identification as mind – to realize this one's true nature.

If it's resistance – it's not me.
This One must let go of resistance – to realize this one's true nature – infinite allowing.

If it's effort – it's not me.
This One must let go of effort – to realize this one's true nature – effortlessness.

If it's impermanent – it's not me.
This One must let go of belief and concept
of impermanence – to realize this one's
true nature – consciousness permanence.

If it's not here now – it's not me.
It it's not one with all that is – it's not me.

Watch the one who is letting go – this is you – the watcher. Watch the one who resists letting go – this is you – the one watching the resisting.

The One Who Sees

Long Version:

It is always now. There is never a time when it is not now. You ask, "What is this 'it' you are referring to?" One answers with silence. Then you ask again, "Please, what is this 'it' I sense?" One answers with stillness. Persistently, a third question beckons, "Please, tell me, what is this 'it' you are making reference to?" No one answers.

As the questioner examines the physical environment to see the one, there is no one there. The questioner raises both arms reaching to the skies - towards infinite outer space above - gasping for breath - to find words that unknowingly muddle inevitable truth - losing the very essence of what the questioner is seeking. Thus, egoic questions of who, what, when, where, why, and how of 'it,' and the 'one' ensue.

As truth begins to emerge, the questioner drops to the ground in despair...sobbing - clawing at the earth. Then, beating the physical ingredients of life with fists of despair, more awakening presents something deep within -

yearning for freedom. A sense of hysterical joy mingled with ironic horror unveils reality - for an instant. A primal scream arises from depths of interdependence of this 'one' which is not separate from ever present eternal nothingness and fullness of 'it' - "WHY!!!!"

Frantically shaking, the cloak of body begins to weaken and fall away. Tears of fear turn to joyous droplets of rain - dissolving back into 'what is' - from whence they came. The "Who am I?" passes through consciousness from unconsciousness where this question has been living...then the question is gone.

The answer seemed to be there, but the nouns and verbs are not. The reason seemed to be there, but the adjectives and adverbs are not. An indescribable knowing is sensed, but the words to share it with others, do not exist, never have, and never will.

Truth awakens further from within and profound essence of nothingness points inward to the inconceivable truth - that no person could ever understand through intellect, thought, memory, or emotion. A realization, "There is no answer." But, 'it' is there - beyond belief - beyond conceptualization - beyond verbalization. "YES!!!!

This one here has seen it! This one here IS IT!!! This one here is - as is all - as is it - as it is...now" "I am...I AM!... I AM!!!!!"

Then..........stillness...........then......nothing..........

then deeper realization……….."There is no then." A deep unshakeable peace and calm arises as truth is fully revealed. This one here sees without eyes, that it is always now - that now is it - and it is one. This one here has awakened. This one here is no longer blind. This one here no longer resists. This one here has let go - surrendered ego - given up the fight – seen itself. This one here is incapable of suffering in any form, for the one is formless. As present as the instant when innocent joy, compassion, and unconditional love breached the womb, yet with vast experience of unknowing, this one here sees….again. I AM all that is - I am life… I am…I…   .

Short Version:

I am like a leaf in the wind…a crashing wave upon the shore…a grain of sand amidst the desert. I am nothing. I am no one. I am. I.   .

About the Author

Charles Rentz, citizen of the USA, was raised in the suburbs of Dayton, Ohio, within the typical American paradigm of conditioning. He recalls, "I remember when I was about four or five years of age, and looking around at my parents and adults, wondering how they were functioning in life – everything seemed so neurotic and counterproductive to peace and happiness." Deep into adulthood, he would later understand that that conscious clarity displayed in childhood became masked with many layers of conditioning and delusion, thereby blocking truth of existence.

Continually adding layer upon layer of untruths, false beliefs, and programming, for the next 3 decades of his life, he continued down the path of the "Typical American," eager to earn a college education, decent job, find a wife, start a family, buy a home, etc. Despite his programming, he never wed nor had any children. He claims there was always a yearning for something more beyond falling into the typical American lifestyle. He shares, "Even though everything I accomplished seemed to always be a huge success, nothing was really fulfilling, deep down. There was always something missing. I felt inauthentic to my own being."

Little did he know what would be unveiled later in his life when he underwent several profound transformations, was an epic shift in awakening consciousness. He shares, "In order to detox from the fast-paced neurotic habits of how I was programmed, trained, and conditioned, I literally had to leave the seemingly self destructive routine of the typical American rat race. I came to a breaking point where I knew, in my heart, that I couldn't play the charade anymore. It was as if I instinctively had to get back to the 'innocence of being' – that whom I was born as – before I was programmed. I had less than $1000 and no idea what I was going to do; but I had to leave."

Charles happened upon a beautiful intentional community, virtually "off the grid," where he was able to devote his full attention to rediscovering himself. He articulates, "It felt like emotional detox, but in truth, many false illusions of myself and the world, and my identities and ego-self, were dissolving." There he discovered that, one day, he would have to entirely let go of who he thinks he is, in order to restore inner peace – relinquish all identities. During that time, he also committed his life to seeking clarity within is own being, first, then if life permits, share his findings with others.

He states that his first book, "Changing the World Without Money or God – A Mindful Journey into Consciousness and Free Thought," was primarily about awareness; he calls it understanding the depths of personal and collective conditioning – a revelation of mind – a deep exploration into how we are unconsciously programmed by culture, religion, and government. However, again, this great accomplishment was not enough, so he continued seeking truth, deeper, within. He intuitively knew the way out of suffering was not to understand the mind, but to transcend it.

Therefore, after a few more years of deep spiritual practice through a variety of disciplines, and for extended periods doing absolutely nothing, he finally surrendered to a journey of awakening. Charles says, "It finally became clear to me, the causal nature of suffering. It is true what the Enlightened Masters are saying, that all suffering arises from being identified with physical form – identification with body and mind. I now know, beyond doubt, there is absolutely a way for suffering to end, completely; and, the option is always here now. That idea was once only theoretical, but I have experienced this transcendence before, and now willing to transcend permanently."

Spanning several years, along his spiritual path, he wrote many pieces of literature which were deeply transformative and vital to gaining conscious clarity. Written in a vastly different style from his first book, Charles decided to share that literature by publishing this book, "Archives of Awakening – A Loving Invitation to Look Within."

Published by

Modern Enlightenment Foundation
Dayton, Ohio 45220

For more information visit:

www.ModernEnlightenmentFoundation.org

www.ingramcontent.com/pod-product-compliance
Lightning Source LLC
Chambersburg PA
CBHW020651300426
44112CB00007B/326